50+ FANDOM PROGRAMS

50+

FANDOM

PROGRAMS

Planning Festivals and Events for Tweens, Teens, and Adults

AMY J. ALESSIO, KATIE LaMANTIA, AND EMILY VINCI

Clifton Park - Halfmoon Public Library
475 Moe Road
Clifton Park, New York 12065

An imprint of the American Library Association
CHICAGO 2017

ISBN: 978-0-8389-1552-3 (paper)

Library of Congress Cataloging-in-Publication Data.
Names: Alessio, Amy J., author. | LaMantia, Katie, author. | Vinci, Emily, 1988- author.
Title: 50+ fandom programs : planning festivals and events for tweens, teens, and adults / Amy J. Alessio, Katie LaMantia, Emily Vinci.
Other titles: Fifty plus fandom programs
Description: Chicago : ALA Editions, an imprint of the American Library Association, 2017. | Includes index.
Identifiers: LCCN 2017002515 | ISBN 9780838915523 (pbk. : alk. paper)
Subjects: LCSH: Libraries—Activity programs—United States. | Young adults' libraries—Activity programs—United States. | Fans (Persons)—Recreation--United States. | Libraries—Special collections—Popular culture. | Libraries—Marketing. | Popular culture—United States.
Classification: LCC Z716.33 .A435 2017 | DDC 027.60973--dc23 LC record available at https://lccn.loc.gov/2017002515

Cover design by Kimberly Thornton. Images © Adobe Stock.
Text design by Alejandra Diaz in the Tisa Pro, Filson Soft, and Nexa Rust Slab typefaces.

♾ This paper meets the requirements of ANSI/NISO Z39.48–1992 (Permanence of Paper).

Printed in the United States of America
21 20 19 18 17   5 4 3 2 1

AA

For my family and for Katie and Emily. Katie has been helping with my crazy program ideas since she was 15, and I'm delighted that Emily has now joined us on these books.

KL

For my family and friends who have always supported me, especially Amy and Emily.

To the library community—you are an inspiration.

EV

For Kit, because he just gets me. ily.

CONTENTS

FESTIVALS AND PROGRAMS

ACKNOWLEDGMENTS

Special thanks to Jamie Santoro and ALA Editions for giving us this opportunity, and to the patrons of the Schaumburg Township District Library for their enthusiasm and participation.

INTRODUCTION

Photos of the Beatles often included fervent, screaming fans. Today fandoms are passionate communities of people that are tied together by their fervent devotion to a fictional book, TV show, movie, game, sport, and more. Nostalgia is often tied to many individuals' devotion to particular fandoms and facets of pop culture.

At the American Library Association's Annual Conference in June 2016 in Orlando, Florida, during a presentation called "The Rise of Fandom in Libraries," the panelists discussed ways in which libraries can engage with fandoms. Although we were not part of that panel, our mission is the same: to provide librarians and library programmers with practical tips and tricks, as well as important concepts and terms to know, that will aid in offering fantastic programs that will appeal to the various fandoms present among your patrons.

THE WORLD OF FANDOM

Fans often search in online communities for other like-minded individuals for support and friendship over a shared interest. Creativity through art and fictional writing based on an original work is commonplace and shared through online forums. Authors and creators vary on permission criteria, but many encourage the shared bonding between fans. (For more information on copyright and creative works, please consult copyright law concerning derivative work.)

Keeping up with popular fandoms is part of the challenge of library service. This book contains basic ideas that can be adapted to lots of fandoms or to programs for different ages. Offering a trivia or fan fiction contest can be a good way to gauge interest before planning a series of events. Or consider adding popular crowd-pleaser elements to a fandom program (for example, including a chocolate tasting during a fantasy book discussion) to discover which interests capture your patrons.

DON'T FORGET PLANNING

When programs have to be planned six to nine months in advance to take advantage of library publicity, it may be necessary to have a pop-up program to capitalize on an interest. Pokémon Go may have been a fad, but it was a huge one that inspired interest in geocaching, Pokémon library interests, and more. The Pokémon fandom grew. Libraries hosted talking tours of Pokémon and other instant events that were publicized online and in-house. Another interest was the Netflix series *Stranger Things*. Libraries had Netflix viewing parties with chats, read-alike displays, and cosplay events. Online publicity has allowed some necessary flexibility in library programming. As libraries respond to more fandoms, they will be better equipped to quickly plan for popular interests.

KEEPING UP WITH TRENDS

It is as important to keep up with fandom trends as it is to stock best-selling authors and movies in the library. Do library missions exist that exclude programming topics that nurture creativity and explore new skills? Likely not. More than a passing fad, interest in a topic so strong that it has a fandom behind it will trigger interest in other library classes and services. For example, steampunk fans could find new authors, movies, costume techniques, and art contests at the library. They will meet other fans and offer suggestions for more programs. For example, they may be particularly interested in making jewelry. The library then can offer more jewelry-making classes and attract patrons beyond the steampunk fans. One fandom can drive new, popular library services.

KNOW YOUR RESOURCES

Many resources are available to help you discover popular fandoms, including Twitter, Tumblr, BuzzFeed, Huffington Post, Reddit, The Mary Sue, Forever Young Adult, *The Fangirl's Guide to the Galaxy* by Sam Maggs, *The Fangirl Life* by Kathleen Smith, and more.

KEY TERMS FOR FANDOMS

The following common terms apply to media sharing, character interests, and more.

- *Memes*: Movies that last a few seconds and that are taken from popular shows and movies to make a point.
- *Gifs*: Still or moving photos.

- *Aesthetics:* A collection of six to twelve photos of a character, a movie, or an author; many involve gifs.
- *Fan fiction:* An author's interpretation using characters and plots created by another author.
- *Canon:* Material taken directly from the source as opposed to an adaptation.
- *Shipping:* Rooting for two characters to fall in love.
- *OTP:* One True Pair; stronger than a ship.

Fandoms can span generations and genders and are often the great equalizer between age and cultural groups. In short, fandoms provide libraries with prime opportunities for unique and exciting programs that will appeal to a wide variety of patrons.

HOW TO USE THIS GUIDE

Programming suggestions for each theme (for example, "Fantastic Favorites" or "Horror and Thrillers") are presented in manageable portions. Many suggestions are listed under each topic so that library programmers may choose ones that work best in different communities. Many activities can be adapted to other themes and programs. Each program will have the following headings where appropriate:

PREP TIME
> This section includes planning and shopping as well as setup time.

LENGTH OF PROGRAM
> This time is a suggestion for a stand-alone event, but more time may be needed to include all activities.

NUMBER OF PATRONS
> This is a suggestion for the number of people attending to make the activities most enjoyable. For example, craft programs should have fewer people if instruction and help will likely be needed.

SUGGESTED AGE RANGE
> This book offers programming suggestions for tweens (ages 10–13), teens (14–19), millennials (20–39), and older adults (40+), although other age ranges may be included now and then. Unless specified, if a program is recommended for millennials, it is not necessarily appropriate for all adults. Millennials like to engage with people who have similar frames of reference for popular culture, just as older adults do. The age ranges are suggested for optimal success of events.

SUPPLIES/SHOPPING

This section lists the items needed for the event. Activities and variations may require additional materials.

ACTIVITIES

This section explains how to run the program and includes setup tips and ideas for experiences to include in programs.

CRAFTS

These activities are designed for the suggested age range.

COSTUMES

If having patrons wear costumes adds to the program, that option will be specified here. Programs that are about costumes or making parts of costumes will not include this additional section.

TRIVIA AND OTHER FREE GAMES

These are easy ways to engage participants in the topic or to build interest before the event.

MARKETING

This section includes techniques and tips for displays and other advertising for each event.

VARIATIONS BY AGE GROUPS

Ways to adapt activities or topics for the different age ranges covered in this book will be listed here.

TIPS AND TRICKS FOR FANDOM EVENTS

The projects and programming suggestions listed in this section can be used with a variety of fandoms and interests. They are go-to ideas for quick planning.

GREEN SCREEN PHOTOS

Get creative and send your patrons home with a memento of your library's fan festival, no matter the occasion! Set up a simple do-it-yourself photo booth with a digital camera and a green fabric backdrop. Then create digital backgrounds and images to transport your fans to their favorite fandom location.

FOODS

Foods for fandom events need not be expensive, though they may sometimes be messy. For many programs, simple cookies from the grocery store can be transformed with ready-made gels or icings. Pipe gel runes for a Shadowhunters cookie-making event, or use different colored gels to signify teams for a sports event. Ask audience members to draw one of the Dancing Men from the famous Sherlock Holmes short story on a cookie or cupcake. Drinks for the Harry Potter butterbeer-making event are messy but fun in small groups.

CRAFTS

Crafts can be as simple as decorating items with markers, such as the capes in the "Cape and Mask Design" event. All ages enjoy coloring, and simple crafts offer not only an enjoyable activity but also the opportunity for participants to take something home. Crafts can also be simplified or eliminated. At least one craft is provided for each theme, and many are interchangeable with other fandom events. Festival events include a wide variety of options and activities so you can choose what will work well with your patrons and space limitations.

For example, more elaborate crafts are included for some programs, such as those described for the "Steampunk It Up" theme, but costs and the availability of supplies have been kept in mind.

TRIVIA

Along with the great love of a fandom usually comes great knowledge of said fandom—and the more obscure and nuanced the knowledge, the better. There's hardly anything die-hard fans (not to be confused with *Die Hard* fans, but probably them, too) love more than showing off their hard-earned knowledge of every nook and cranny of their pop culture obsession.

MULTIMEDIA FUN

Remix and re-create favorite scenes from movies, TV shows, and more using library software you have on hand. Use digital cameras or computers to film stop-motion animation scenes with toys or LEGOs. Remix trailers from favorite fandoms, or give them a twist.

FAN ART AND EDITS

Whether it's holding a flash fan fiction contest or a fan art show-and-tell, giving your patrons a chance to show off the ways in which they express their fandom never hurts! You can include time for sharing fan fiction and fan art at a lot of different programs—a library mini con, a program related to a specific superhero or TV series or movie, or even a gaming program.

GAMING

Gaming provides a variety of options for every type of player, whether it's video gaming, tabletop, role-playing (RPG), MMORPG (massive multiplayer online role-playing game), or a combination. Incorporating gaming into your fandom festival is a great way to make it more interactive and challenging and to introduce players to new and exciting games.

MOVIEOKE

Movieoke is a great way to add an interactive, low-cost element to your program. Invite your attendees to test their memories as well as their acting chops with movie scene karaoke. We all say, "I'm not wearing hockey pants" while we watch *The Dark Knight* anyway, right? If you feel your attendees might need some motivation, hold a contest and give a prize to the best movieoke-er!

COSPLAY

No longer just for teens, cosplay appeals to all ages, and everyone can enjoy events with cosplay activities built in. Options for adults to wear costumes of some sort are described in most of the festival themes in this book. Including cosplay does not necessarily mean that the event becomes more complicated. Offering a photo area or green screen with themed backgrounds (and having staff e-mail pictures to attendees) can work with most of the programs described in this book, including the sports ones! Or staff can just provide a photo op area and a place for audience members to post their pictures online while tagging the library. Parades through the library are optional if participating adults are interested, or a special thirty- to forty-five-minute cosplay gathering at the end of a festival allows everyone to enjoy costumes while meeting others interested in the same fandom.

MAKEUP

Consider buying some makeup kits on sale after Halloween to have on hand for some of your fandom events. Or use traditional makeup in new ways. For example, attendees can use eyebrow pencils or temporary tattoo markers to draw Shadowhunter runes on their faces, necks, or hands. Wearable comic art can include small logos. Sports fans always find creative ways to show their team spirit. A makeup station with disposable applicators may add another fun activity to some of the themed programs.

3-D DESIGN AND PRINTING

If your library has access to a 3-D printer, use it for your fandom programs. Prints of popular characters or easily recognizable items can be made on a 3-D printer and used for scavenger hunts. Creating items on a 3-D printer is also a fun and unique way to market fandom programs at outreach events. In addition, 3-D prints can replace tabletop pieces for gaming events, and attendees can design their own. The possibilities are endless.

CHECKLIST FOR SUCCESS!

Large-scale programs are often, if not always, a team effort. Here are our tried-and-true tips for a winning programming team.

- *Create a shared spreadsheet or document to track expenses.* This approach is especially helpful if you are pulling money from multiple budgets and need to keep track of the total amount spent on each project by individual departments. Use the spreadsheet to keep track of quantities ordered and used and performers hired; it can also be used to justify potential future budget increases.

- *Use an online form for all library staff to make suggestions about a fandom festival.* Such a form allows all departments to have buy-in and provides an opportunity for feedback from those not directly involved in programming. Library staff have diverse interests and great ideas, and this form is a way to reach out to talented staff and let everyone have a voice. Many nonprogrammers may have a particular affinity for a certain fandom that other library staff may not be aware of and can use their knowledge to benefit the library and the program. All staff members can contribute ideas and provide input, even if they choose not to be directly involved with event planning. The online idea form can be modified to be anonymous if you prefer.

- *Allow more than one person to be in charge of meetings.* Rotate who is in charge and who facilitates planning the meetings, taking notes, and choosing the agenda.

- *Share your information with your planning group.* Use project software and include contacts, meeting agendas, event ideas, and the final event outline. This shared information guarantees that group members know clearly what their assignments are and where people will be during the festival. Multiple web-based project management tools are available, including Basecamp and Google Drive.

- *Inform staff at all public desks that the festival is occurring!* Although your event likely appeared in your library's program guide or newsletter, it is a good idea to send a reminder e-mail to staff close to the date depending on how much turnout you anticipate. How early you want to inform staff members depends on your library's size, but we recommend at least one week ahead of time. Once the schedule of activities is finalized, send it out to all staff, especially if your festival spans multiple rooms and departments.

- *Give public desk staff something fun to wear, decorate, or pass out to patrons.* For example, encourage cosplay or costumes during a comic con or add house colors to circulation desks during the week leading up to a Harry Potter festival. Decorations, costumes, or handouts give nonprogrammers a stake in a library event and an opportunity to become active participants. Such staff involvement is also a great way to market your programs to patrons and to promote events just by spurring conversations about decorations or costumes.

- *Create a list of performers and the staff members they should contact when they arrive.* This list will eliminate confusion about whom to contact and which phone numbers to use. If it is likely that staff members will not be at their desks near their phones, consider listing cell phone numbers so that performers can contact the correct staff member directly.

- *Make sure backup activities are available.* In case a performer cancels, a room is suddenly unavailable, or another unexpected circumstance pops up, you will need to regroup quickly. See the "Tips and Tricks for Fandom Events" section for more resources that can be put together on the fly.

- *Follow up with staff and performers by sending thank-you e-mails or notes.* Thank staff for their positive attitudes and extra help during the event. If this event was new and being tried for the first time, include positive patron interactions and statistics. For performers, be sure to include statistics about the turnout and let them know whether you'd like them to return next year. Don't forget to include pictures from the day!

- *Evaluate your program.* Develop evaluation questions for patrons to answer at the program, or send evaluation forms to patrons later. Evaluations can be two to three simple questions and should be specific for your library. Think about your goals for each program or festival and what you hope patrons will learn by attending.

FESTIVALS AND PROGRAMS

NOW FOR THE FUN PART. The remainder of this book will offer ways to explore patron passions about a wide variety of topics from history to sports to popular culture. Some programs are elaborate, some may involve an entire day or several days of events, and some are very simple.

Level 7

CROSSOVER PARTIES

THE EVENTS IN THIS SECTION cover genres or trends that can include multiple fandoms. Offering one of these events will help reveal patrons' interest in other fandoms. For example, the "50 Shades of Hot Books" program could appeal to fans of the Victorian or Medieval period. A lot of interest in Medieval historical romance titles could then lead to more program planning relating to that period. "Mystery Mayhem" offers suspenseful activities that Sherlock Holmes fans may enjoy. Those Sherlock Holmes fans may then want to look at the different actors in those movies, giving Sherlock his own fandom later in this guide (see "Sherlock Fest"). The "What's Trending?" program helps libraries plan events when a new Netflix or television series gains momentum quickly.

50 SHADES OF HOT BOOKS

People should not be embarrassed about what they read, and those who like hot reads will enjoy attending this event with other fans of the genre. Celebrate hot books and romantic stories as the last 50 Shades movie is released or around Valentine's Day.

PREP TIME	LENGTH OF PROGRAM	NUMBER OF PATRONS	SUGGESTED AGE RANGE
3 hours	90 minutes	30	Millennials and older adults

Supplies/Shopping

CHOCOLATE FONDUE

- Milk chocolate chips
- Half-and-half (cream)
- Strawberries
- Potato chips
- Graham crackers
- Marshmallows
- Pound cake, cut into cubes
- Bananas
- Plates
- Spoons
- Napkins
- Sparkling grape juice
- Paper cups or plastic champagne glasses

BOARD GAMES

- M&Ms and small paper cups for HEART Bingo
- A couple of copies of games about dating, marriage, and life, such as Mystery Date and Life

HAVE A HEART NECKLACES

- Silver chains with clasps
- Heart charms or large heart-shaped rings
- Silver jump rings
- Silver eye pins or T-pins
- Red, pink, black, and purple medium-sized beads
- Wire cutters
- Long- and short-nose pliers
- Candy prizes (optional)

Activities

- As people arrive, have them write a favorite romance author (or a favorite author or book) on the sign-in sheet. Have romantic music playing. Read the authors and titles after everyone is seated (without saying who liked which author) so people may have some suggestions to take home.

- *Romance in Chocolate:* Serve chocolate fondue and sparkling grape juice. As participants sample the different dipping options, have them vote on their favorites.

- *Musical Romance:* Play short excerpts of love songs, and ask participants to guess the titles. Play songs from several different musical eras.

- *50 Kinds of Romance:* Review several types of romance books in a presentation showing the covers. Provide a list of titles on a handout for audience members to take home. Provide some pencils so people can add other ideas. The list should include diverse authors and at least three books in several categories from sweet to scorching, including inspirational, historical, Western, hot contemporary, humorous, erotic, 50 Shades read-alikes, Highlander, time travel (e.g., Outlander), and other popular genres.

- *Vote for Romance:* Ask participants to suggest the most romantic movie, TV show scene, or kiss and then have the group vote.

- *LOVEly Board Games:* Invite audience members to play HEART Bingo with M&M markers. Make boards with book titles or use regular numbered cards and provide candy prizes.

- If there is time, audience members can play Mystery Date and Life while enjoying each other's company.

Crafts

- *Have a Heart Necklaces:* These simple necklaces can be made by putting charms and a couple of beads on jump rings or pins and attaching them to the chains. Necklaces can have three pins that slide freely on the chains.

Trivia and Other Free Games

- *Match the Lyric to the Song:* Read love song lyrics and ask audience members to guess the song.

Marketing

- Put large, red lip prints on bookmarks with program information printed on them and place the bookmarks in your romance books to advertise the event.

- Print information about the program on small slips of paper and wrap them around mini chocolate bars to hand out in the days before the event.

Variations by Age Groups

- *Tweens and teens:* A booklist featuring titles on different types of love, including love for family and friends, could be used at this program for younger readers. Or choose some of the crafts and snacks for a Fond of Chocolate Fest. The Have a Heart Necklaces will appeal to younger ages, along with the fondue, HEART Bingo, and board games.

▶ MYSTERY MAYHEM

Mystery evenings and escape rooms are growing in popularity. Mystery activities can be simple, and escape room games can be purchased and adapted for libraries. Some activities from the "Sherlock Fest" program can be crossovers for a mystery event, too, including the puzzle competitions and the puzzle-piece jewelry and keychains.

PREP TIME	LENGTH OF PROGRAM	NUMBER OF PATRONS	SUGGESTED AGE RANGE
4 hours (for escape room activity setup)	3 hours	25	14+

Supplies/Shopping

- Chocolate (several flavors)
- Potato chips (several flavors)
- Plates
- Napkins

ESCAPE ROOM

- Many supplies and props are needed for the escape room. A purchased kit will help with planning. See also the websites in the "Activities" section.

Activities

These activities can be done in one room while a few people at a time are in the escape room for their fifteen-minute game.

- *Solve a Crime Scene:* Rope or tape off an area of the floor. Inside the marked-off area, make a messy crime scene using objects at hand: an overturned chair, a phone, lipstick, a shoe, gloves, any unusual item from the library. As people arrive, invite them to describe what happened on a sheet of paper. Award a small prize for most creative, shortest, most likely, and so on.

- *Mystery Flavors:* Pass out unusual flavors of chocolate or potato chips one at a time on plates. Have participants guess what the flavors are and choose their favorite ones.

- *Escape Room:* Consider asking local escape room sites (more are popping up continually) to help set up a game at the library. Other options are outlined in the following websites, but purchased kits and other scenarios need to be made specific to library situations. If no locked room is available, some libraries substitute quests, such as Find the Treasure.

- ‣ https://americanlibrariesmagazine.org/2016/09/01/escape-rooms -libraries-on-lockdown/
- ‣ www.teenlibrariantoolbox.com/2016/07/tpib-locked-in-the-library

Crafts

- *Mystery Craft:* Pull craft supplies from the library closets, including lots of paper, yarn, duct tape, scissors, markers, and more. Have a kit at each table. Give participants five minutes to make something out of the craft supplies, including a hat, a bag, a shoe, a wallet, or a weapon.

Trivia and Other Free Games

- *Two-Minute Mysteries:* Between activities, read some one- or two-minute mysteries from books or online sources and have participants solve them.

Marketing

- Place footprints on the floor leading to the event to indicate a mystery program.
- Place a masking tape outline of a body near a display of mystery books and movies.

Variations by Age Groups

- *Tweens and teens—Life-Sized Clue:* Many libraries have offered a life-sized version of Clue. This program requires the help of volunteers but is lots of fun. The *Green Bean Teen Queen* blog has an in-depth description of a successful event (www.greenbeanteenqueen.com/2012/11/library -programs-life-size-clue.html).

- *All ages—Guest CSI Speaker:* Ask your local police personnel to demonstrate what a CSI officer or the K-9 unit does. Some mystery authors also may be good speakers about forensic evidence if any are available locally.

- *Older adults—Mystery Puzzles:* Invite groups to put together 100 piece puzzles without an illustration to guide them.

⬡ WHAT'S TRENDING?

Host a pop-up fandom event for a new movie, Netflix, or media series. Pop culture happens at lightning speed, and new crazes can appear overnight. Because of the advanced planning required to get library events listed in program guides and newsletters, it may seem like cashing in on an instant success isn't possible. Pop-up programs, however, have become popular, in part as a way to do relevant pop culture programming while that piece of pop culture is, in fact, still relevant. The following isn't a strict guide for how to hold a pop-up pop culture program; rather, we list things to keep in mind when planning a program around what's trending.

Activities

The activities you plan will depend, of course, on the subject of your program. The point isn't necessarily for these programs to be extensive or highly involved but instead to be fun and engaging. Rather than requiring registration, consider doing drop-in programs. With a drop-in format, participants don't need to come at an exact start time and stay until the end. Depending on your space availabilies, consider setting up tables in the lobby or even outside the library in places that get a lot of patron traffic.

Crafts

Crafts are a great spur-of-the-moment, low-key activity. Crafts are also a great option if your library (perhaps your children's department) has a stock of crafting supplies.

Costumes

A costume contest is a fun and different way to engage your patrons. Have them dress up as their favorite character from the latest breakout hit, and award prizes to the winners!

Trivia and Other Free Games

Although the latest hit show might not have been around long enough for there to be a wealth of trivia questions about it, consider holding a pop-up trivia program that involves some of the subject matter involved in the show (or movie or game) that your program is focused on. For example, if the show takes place during a particular decade, your questions can be related to the pop culture of that decade.

Marketing

Because this program will be done very soon and, therefore, likely won't make it into many of your library's marketing materials, internal marketing such as displays and posters as well as external marketing on your library's website and social media will be particularly important.

Variations by Age Groups

Variations aren't necessary because the hope is that this program will appeal to any and all fans of the latest craze!

FANTASTIC FAVORITES

FANTASY AND SUSPENSE FANS WILL find plenty to enjoy with these programs, which inspire creativity, bend brains, or offer escape and enjoyment. Although the "Creature Creations" and "Fan Fiction" programs could appeal to fans of several fantasy series, the "Game of Thrones," "Shadowhunters Library Institute," and "Sherlock Fest" programs will tie in directly to specific books and pop culture.

◉ CREATURE CREATIONS

Fantasy creatures have always been essential to the world building and development of immersive stories, especially in fantasy book series. Where would we be without dragons, chimeras, mermaids, and hobbits to enrich our stories? These fanciful beings leave the door wide open to many possibilities for creative programs, even if patrons aren't familiar with every creature and literary reference.

PRO TIP

Use this program with your Writing Club for a fun 3-D prompt exercise outside the ordinary.

PREP TIME	LENGTH OF PROGRAM	NUMBER OF PATRONS	SUGGESTED AGE RANGE
2 hours	2 hours	15–20	Tweens+

Supplies/Shopping

- Modeling clay
- Toothpicks
- Acrylic paint
- Paintbrushes
- Rolling pins or food cans
- Plush toys, dolls
- Safety pins
- Sewing kits
- Scissors

Activities

- *Frankenstein's Lab:* Patrons become Dr. Frankenstein and design their very own creatures in the library's laboratory. Buy plush toys and dolls from a secondhand or dollar store, cut them apart, and have participants use safety pins or sewing kits to reassemble bits and pieces in a unique (and horrifying) operation. This activity can be especially timely around Halloween.

- *Collectible Creatures:* Participants can paint figurines and collectibles of fierce fantasy creatures to take home. Ask patrons to raid their closets and bring in old creature figurines to repaint. Alternatively, partner with a gaming shop and ask whether the operator knows of any expert refinishers who would demonstrate techniques or donate fantasy game pieces.

Crafts

- *Clay Creatures:* Participants can design fantastical creatures out of modeling clay, creating either an entirely new beast or something from a book they've read. Provide toothpicks and rolling pins or food cans to help patrons model the clay better. Ask patrons why they chose their particular creature or specific features. If there is time, use the creatures to create a stop-motion animation story.

Trivia and Other Free Games

- *Name That Creature:* Participants can identify the creature that goes with a popular book or a movie or TV series. This game can also be an interactive display with signs that patrons can flip up on a wall. Patrons can guess the creature and fandom shown on the front page and then lift up the page to discover if they are correct on the second page.

Marketing

- Ask to hang up fliers at your local comic book, gaming, and collectibles shops, especially if you are partnering for the program.

- Create a "local collectibles" display of fantastical creatures from patrons, staff, or a gaming shop.

- There is a great crossover potential for the world of J. K. Rowling's creatures in *Fantastic Beasts and Where to Find Them* and the Harry Potter books. Consider marketing these ideas and program elements together.

Variations by Age Groups

- *Millennials and older adults:* The creatures in Dungeons and Dragons (D&D) are extremely vast and offer so many possibilities that an entire program could be focused on them alone. If you have an active D&D group at your library or local comics shop, consider offering a 3-D design class for people to create their own characters and creatures they may encounter throughout their campaigns.

- *Tweens and teens:* Design comfy and fashionable life-sized mermaid tails that double as blankets. This project may seem challenging, but patterns are available for free online, and the tails can be made without sewing. Use fleece blanket materials and, instead of sewing, tie off the blankets on both sides of the fins, similar to tied blankets. If your library has sewing machines, put them to good use, but make sure that tweens and teens are trained to use them and that extra staff are on hand.

▶ FAN FICTION

Fans express their devotion and involvement in their fandoms in a variety of ways, and fan fiction is certainly one of them. Fan fiction generally involves generating original stories using the characters and universe created by an author. This practice has existed far longer than one might think, but it gained considerable steam with the advent of the Internet and sites like fanfiction.net and Archive of Our Own. This program is intended to give patrons a chance to share their writing (if they want to) and to learn from one another.

PREP TIME	LENGTH OF PROGRAM	SUGGESTED AGE RANGE
2 hours	1½ hours	Tweens and teens

Number of Patrons

15 (The number of patrons for this program is intentionally smaller than that for most other programs to reduce the intimidation factor that many young writers—and all writers, really—are prone to facing.)

Supplies/Shopping

No supplies are necessary, but keep in mind that treats make great writing fuel!

Activities

The suggested activities are all intended for small-group events, and, depending on what you have in mind for your specific program, you can choose the one(s) that will work best.

- *Intro to Fan Fiction:* What is fan fiction? Patrons may have heard of it, maybe have even read it, but aren't sure how to go about writing it for themselves. You can go over common terms associated with fan fiction as well as review resources for writing and sharing. In addition, if some patrons in attendance have experience writing fan fic, they can share tips and tricks.

- *Peer Editing:* Participants can workshop pieces they are working on and get feedback from their peers.
- *Writing Prompts:* You can give participants writing prompts for inspiration—for example, "Your character [whomever participants have chosen to focus their writing on] shows up in [the town in which you're located]. Write a story about the character's experiences from that character's perspective." This exercise is particularly great for those just getting started writing fan fic.

Marketing

- Create a display of popular titles (books as well as movie and TV series) that inspire fan fiction (e.g., Harry Potter, Star Trek, Star Wars, Supernatural, Twilight, and the like) along with writing manuals and books about fandom. Include information about the program on the display.

Variations by Age Groups

- *Millennials:* A similar program can be held for millennials and older adults, but it is probably best to keep it as a separate program due to the potential adult nature of some of the writing.

● GAME OF THRONES

Game of Thrones became a cultural phenomenon for millennials and adults of all ages when the TV series premiered in 2011. Based on the popular book series by George R. R. Martin, *Game of Thrones* has become a water-cooler subject at work, at school, and among friends. *Game of Thrones* captures more than just fantasy; it embodies the human struggle, incorporating political challenges, amazing cinematography, and intricate storytelling. Capture the popularity by hosting a viewing party or fan night to celebrate everything from dragons to wildfire.

PREP TIME	LENGTH OF PROGRAM	NUMBER OF PATRONS	SUGGESTED AGE RANGE
2–3 hours	2 hours	20–30	Millennials and older adults

Supplies/Shopping

- Wooden doorstops
- Paint
- Markers
- Paintbrushes
- Name tags
- Styrofoam eggs
- Thumbtacks
- Nail polish (assorted bright colors)
- Glue
- Green screen
- Camera
- Green screen props
- Punch bowls
- Plates
- Snacks
- Cups
- Napkins

Activities

- Although not necessary, themed snacks are great for this program: Red (velvet) Wedding cupcakes, Wildfire punch, chocolate dragon eggs, Sansa's favorite lemon cakes, and sparkling grape juice (don't tell Joffrey it's poisoned).

- Set up a green screen photo booth and transport your patrons to Westeros. Provide props, such as baby dragon stuffed animals, crowns, and plastic swords, and let patrons sit on the Iron Throne before they meet an untimely end as King or Queen. Provide four or five backgrounds for patrons to select from and either e-mail digital copies or print out copies on-site if possible.

- *Game of Thrones Inspired Hair:* Participants can learn how to style their hair in the intricate braids of the *Game of Thrones* women. Invite local cosmetology students to test their skills, or partner with a local salon.

- *Game of Thrones Dragon Match:* Have a book versus TV show discussion and debate. Ask patrons to make predictions about the series, and post the predictions on social media. These predictions can spark lively debate and conversation.

> **PRO TIP**
>
> If you choose to have a viewing party and want to watch an episode, check with your library director first about licensing agreements and graphic content.

Crafts

- *"Hold-the-Door" Doorstops:* In honor of Hodor and his (spoiler alert) sacrifice, attendees can take home their own doorstops. Purchase wooden doorstops from a local hardware store or online and have participants decorate the doorstops with paint or markers.

- *Dragon Eggs:* Participants can design their own dragon eggs using Styrofoam eggs and flathead thumbtacks. In case some thumbtacks don't stick, have glue available for patrons. Provide bright colors of nail polish for painting the eggs once completed.

Trivia and Other Free Games

- Challenge patrons to identify Houses by their sigils and words in a matching game or through traditional trivia open-ended questions and answers.

- Create large-scale family trees from the noble Houses for participants to work on as a collaborative project. Find out how far back patrons can go and where the families intertwine. It may be best to focus on a few of the main families (Lannister, Stark, Baratheon, and the like).

- Participants can discover their *Game of Thrones* name and House with an online generator, or people can get creative and come up with their own! Have patrons use these names on their name tags for a fun conversation starter.

Marketing

- If you have an adult fiction book club, read the first book in the series before your *Game of Thrones* program. Place promotional materials or stickers in the book club copies.

- Set the date for the *Game of Thrones* program to coincide with the date of the premiere of the TV show or next book release.

- Use imagery and iconic words from the series, such as "Winter Is Coming," and depict the Iron Throne in your promotional materials. Advertise near your science fiction shelves and in the audiovisual area near TV series.

Variations by Age Groups

- *Tweens and teens:* Although many tweens and teens are not watching or reading the series yet, many know the interest and pop culture standards it holds in the world. Some elements of *Game of Thrones,* such as swordplay, can be used with a medieval program. Another crossover possibility is a "March Madness" program designed as a competition for the Iron Throne.

● SHADOWHUNTERS LIBRARY INSTITUTE

Train Shadowhunters fans at this Library Institute. Cassandra Clare's intertwining series and the TV show fuel enthusiasm for the Shadowhunters series. Steam-punk activities would be a good crossover with this event because The Infernal Devices trilogy is in that genre.

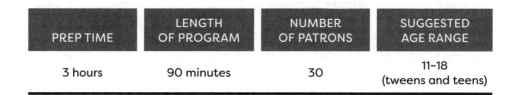

PREP TIME	LENGTH OF PROGRAM	NUMBER OF PATRONS	SUGGESTED AGE RANGE
3 hours	90 minutes	30	11–18 (tweens and teens)

Supplies/Shopping

CHURCH'S MYSTERIOUS FLAVORED GOLDFISH

- Goldfish crackers in at least five flavors
- Small plates
- Napkins or paper towels

RUNE SNACKS

- Plain cupcakes or cookies
- Decorating gel tubes
- Frosting
- Plastic knives
- Small plates
- Napkins or paper towels

RUNE STEAMPUNK JEWELRY OR KEYCHAINS

- Keychain hardware
- Silver link chains (at least 22 inches long)
- Gear charms (a lot, at least three or four per participant; assorted metallics)
- Jump rings in silver and bronze, medium-sized to go around gears and chain links
- Wire cutters, long- and short-nose pliers (at least three sets of tools)
- Beading craft wire (silver, 20 gauge)

MORTAL CUP DECORATION

- Plastic wine glasses
- Metallic gold Sharpies (at least six)

STELE CRAFT

(www.instructables.com/id/Mortal-Instruments-How-to-Make-a-Stele
-Pen/?ALLSTEPS)

- Pens or markers
- Wooden dowel rods
- Packing tape
- Duct tape (optional)
- Silver paint
- Black Sharpie
- Scissors

MORTAL INSTRUMENTS ACTIVITIES

- Photocopied pages from the Mortal Instruments coloring book
- Colored pencils
- Rune stones
- Handout or book about runes

MEMORY RUNE GAME

- Photocopies of runes
- Pencils
- Paper
- Ink-jet printer
- Laptop
- Printable tattoo sheets for ink-jet printers

RUNE OR QUOTE TATTOOS

- Tattoo paper
- Laptop or computer access
- Ink-jet printer

PRIZES AND HANDOUTS

- Small, glittery notebooks for prizes (optional)
- Set of rune stones (optional)
- Bags to take crafts home

Activities and Crafts

- Make a sample Mortal Cup with a gold Sharpie and plastic wine glass. Hide it in the room or out in the library. Set up the crafts at stations in the room: ink-jet printer plus tattoo paper and laptop; cupcakes or cookies, knives, plates, tubes of decorating gel, and frosting; stele-making supplies; keychain and jewelry supplies.

- *Church's Mysterious Flavored Goldfish:* This activity is the opening ice breaker. As participants enter, give each person a small plate. When everyone is seated, pass around one flavor of Goldfish crackers at a time and have patrons rate it on a scale of 1 to 5, with 5 being delicious and 1 being a flavor they hate. Patrons also have to guess what each flavor is. This activity is just for fun, so if participants are talking among themselves, it's fine.

- *Memory Rune Game:* Copy several runes from the Codex or from the Shadowhunters Wiki. Place one set of runes on each table along with pencils and blank paper. Have everyone look at the runes for thirty seconds and then quickly collect the photocopies. Participants have to draw and label as many runes from memory as they can.

- Invite participants to work in small groups at each of the following five stations, switching stations every fifteen minutes.
    - *Rune or Quote Tattoos:* Participants can find Cassandra Clare quotes and runes online and print them on the tattoo paper. Groups should put as many runes as possible on one sheet before printing.
    - *Rune Snacks:* Using gel decorating tubes and frosting, patrons can decorate cupcakes or cookies with runes.
    - *Rune Steampunk Jewelry or Keychains:* Using jump rings, participants can attach gear charms to the chains or keychains. If patrons can bend wires into runes, those can be attached as well. The Angelic Power rune is likely the easiest to do.
    - *Mortal Cup Decoration:* Using gold metallic Sharpie pens, participants can decorate their own Mortal Cups.
    - *Stele Craft:* Following the Instructable website directions, help patrons break the dowel rods and tape them to the pens. They can make raised runes with duct tape or paint the stele pens and then add runes with the black Sharpies.

- After participants complete the five stations, they can color sheets from the Mortal Instruments coloring book or look at rune stones. Put out the rune stones with a book or handout explaining basic meanings.

- When patrons are finished with crafts and projects, invite them to go look for the Mortal Cup. The person who finds it could win a copy of the coloring book or another prize.

- Hand out Magnus's glittery notebooks as participants leave.

Costumes

- Provide makeup crayons or eyebrow pencils for those who do not come with runes applied. Be sure to wipe the crayons or pencils with alcohol between uses.

Trivia and Other Free Games

- Create a simple Jeopardy! competition with book, movie, and TV show categories. Books can be divided by series, and you could have a category for Cassandra Clare's coauthors, too.

Marketing

- Display runes prominently by the books and at the teen and youth services desks to get the attention of potential attendees.

Variations by Age Groups

- *Millennials—Movie Night:* Fans in their 20s grew up reading Cassandra Clare's books and may enjoy a fandom night. Before showing the movie, have participants decorate the plastic wine cups and then pour sparkling grape juice. Attendees can paint or draw a cover of one of the books, such as *Lady Midnight,* while sipping and watching the movie.

- *Millennials—Coffee Foam Runes:* Another activity for millennials is to make runes out of coffee foam. Have participants try making runes using instant espresso and a foamer with milk.

- *All ages—Quote Shirts or Calligraphy:* Demonstrate some basic calligraphy styles and invite fans to write some quotes from the books using calligraphy pens. Or quotes can be printed on iron-on transfers and used to decorate tote bags or T-shirts, along with runes.

- *All ages—Self-Defense Moves:* Participants can train like a Shadowhunter by learning some basic self-defense moves. A martial artist can help with this activity, which could last thirty minutes. Participants can also break thin boards and then decorate the pieces with runes.

- *All ages:* Hand out a list of online resources for displaying or selling fan art. Discuss where fan fiction is published. Host a fan art display in the library after the event or hold a fan fiction contest.

● SHERLOCK FEST

With new stars appearing in fresh Sherlock Holmes movies and television shows, interest in the popular mystery series remains constant. A mystery and Sherlock Holmes fest will offer fun ways to share the favorite sleuth's stories with other fans.

PREP TIME	LENGTH OF PROGRAM	NUMBER OF PATRONS	SUGGESTED AGE RANGE
2 hours	60 to 90 minutes	25	Millennials and older adults

Supplies/Shopping

- 5 jigsaw puzzles with 100–250 pieces (either five copies of the same puzzle or five similar puzzles with the same number of pieces)
- 1 used puzzle that is missing pieces (the pieces will be used for a craft) or a puzzle from a thrift store
- Paper
- Pencils or pens
- Dancing Men code sheet
- Jump rings
- Wire cutters
- Long-nose pliers
- Earring wires
- Keychain hardware
- 1 straight pin (to make holes in puzzle pieces)
- Instant coffee and tea packets
- Cups for hot drinks
- Almond cookies and fortune cookies
- Chocolate (several flavors)
- Plates
- Napkins

Activities

- *Notice Your Neighbor:* As people arrive, have classical violin music playing. Invite participants to taste the first packet of instant coffee or tea. Ask them to introduce themselves to the people at their table (allow five minutes for these introductions). Then ask patrons to switch tables randomly so they are sitting with new people. Pass out paper and pencils and ask attendees to write as many details as they can about the people they met at the first table.

- *Dancing Men Code:* Hand out a message made with the code from "The Adventure of the Dancing Men." If participants cannot make headway after a few minutes, hand out the code sheet.

- *Falls Fiction:* Ask one person at each table to write a few sentences describing what might have happened to Holmes and Moriarty over the Falls. That person should then pass the paper to the right. Each person adds one sentence until everyone at the table has contributed. Periodically invite participants to taste and guess the various tea or coffee flavors.

- *The Quick Crime:* In a prearranged scenario, have another staff member run in and take your purse or phone before dashing out again. Ask audience members to describe and draw the staff member as accurately as possible.

- *Puzzle Tournament:* Which table of five people can solve their puzzle the fastest?

- *Which Sherlock?:* Show the last five minutes (or up to the announcement of the solution) of *The Hound of the Baskervilles* with three versions of Sherlock: Basil Rathbone, Richard Roxburgh, and Benedict Cumberbatch.

- *Or Which Watson?:* Show a few minutes of Watson depictions, including Joan Watson in the television show *Elementary*.

- *Discuss Preferences:* Read the last page of "A Study in Pink," when Sherlock and Watson decide to go out for Chinese food, and serve the cookies.

Crafts

- *Puzzle-Piece Earrings or Keychains:* Have participants use straight pins to punch a hole in each puzzle piece (use the incomplete puzzle). Using jump rings, attendees then can attach the puzzle pieces to keychains or earrings.

Costumes

- People who come in costume can receive a small prize.

Trivia and Other Free Games

- Holmes trivia games abound online. Use questions between activities.

Marketing

- Place footprints leading to a display of Doyle books plus Holmes read-alikes and variations. Include program information or fliers in the display.

Variations by Age Groups

- *Tweens:* Several middle-grade Holmes read-alikes are available now. Have attendees read one of several choices and then talk about what they liked. You could ask them to read a short story, too, and compare it with the book. Show the Dancing Men code and have participants make and translate messages. Then offer the puzzle competition as well as the jewelry and keychain making. Have participants taste the chocolate and identify the mysterious flavors.

- *Millennials:* Show one of the Robert Downey Jr. Sherlock Holmes films as a crossover with steampunk activities.

GOTTA GAME!

ALL AGES ENJOY GAMING. MATCH gaming interests to different communities with the variety of ideas in this section. From "Big Board Games" to "Old-School Video Games," there is something for everyone here. Special interests can be found in the "Dungeons and Dragons" program or in "Magic: The Gathering."

⬢ BIG BOARD GAMES

Tabletop gaming is fun, but bringing to life your favorite board games takes gaming to the next level! Transform your library (or just a room or two) into Gaming Central with big board games that you can create and play on a large scale. Games that typically were limited to patrons sitting at a table and moving pieces can be transformed as patrons now become the pieces in a game. The possibilities are nearly limitless.

Raid your board game closet and see what games might be good to play on a larger scale. Decide if you want to focus your program on one specific life-sized board game or multiple life-sized board games and how many rooms you want to (or can) take up in your library. Think about involving your Teen Advisory Board or Friends group to create or run the games if you choose to have multiple games or to have a large-scale event for all ages or for children. Some easy games to re-create on a large scale are Hungry Hungry Hippos, Pac-Man, and Chutes and Ladders.

PREP TIME	LENGTH OF PROGRAM	NUMBER OF PATRONS
5 hours	1–3 hours	Dependent on number of players per game

Suggested Age Range

All ages (Big board games can be adapted for any age group, but try to group players of similar ages in the same rounds.)

Supplies/Shopping

HUMAN HUNGRY HUNGRY HIPPOS

- Ball pit balls (large bag of plastic balls, 200+)
- Scooters (or chairs with wheels)
- Small, plastic laundry baskets
- Masking tape

PAC-MAN

- Masking tape or painter's tape
- White bedsheets
- Colored paper or plastic gold coins or chocolate coins

CHUTES AND LADDERS

- Construction paper (red, yellow, blue, and green)
- Toy rope ladders or thick twine or masking tape
- Balance boards or two-by-fours
- Masking or duct tape
- Spinner from a Twister game (If you don't have one available, you can borrow a spinner from another game or create your own either online or out of card stock and cardboard.)

Activities

Set up multiple rooms of life-sized games for patrons to enjoy, or focus on one life-sized game for a specific age group.

HUMAN HUNGRY HUNGRY HIPPOS

Setup
- Place a scooter or a chair with wheels and a plastic laundry basket in each corner of a large, empty room.

- Place a long piece of masking tape in each corner to determine each team's home base where team members will keep their winnings each round.

How to Play
- Create four teams consisting of three players each. Player 1 will be the ball catcher, or the Human Hungry Hungry Hippo. Player 1 kneels or sits cross-legged on the scooter or chair and collects as many plastic balls as possible in the laundry basket without using her hands to grab them. Player 1 must place the laundry basket upside down to trap the plastic balls while remaining on the scooter or chair. Player 2 pushes Player 1 by the shoulders to the center of the room where the plastic balls will be dispersed. Player 3 remains behind the masking tape line at home base to collect the team's winnings. Each round should last two to three minutes, depending on how many balls you have.

- After each round, rotate the players on each team so everyone gets to try a new position. If you have access to a whiteboard, keep track of each team's scores. If you notice players are collecting the balls too quickly, keep a few balls back and roll them into the middle of the room near the end of the game.

PAC-MAN

Setup

- Create a grid layout similar to that of the original Pac-Man using masking tape for the interior and exterior outlines. Strategically place crumpled-up colored paper to use as dots on the interior walkways. (You can substitute plastic gold coins for the dots, or use chocolate coins for a tasty treat!) Secure the dots with tape on the bottom. Cut holes in white bedsheets for helpers who are ghosts.

How to Play

- Place your designated ghosts in the middle of the game. Pac-Men can start from any of the openings. For each step a Pac-Man takes, the player collects the dots while avoiding being tagged by the ghosts. The goal is to be the last Pac-Man remaining while collecting the most dots.

CHUTES AND LADDERS

Setup

- Lay out different-colored pieces of construction paper on the floor to form a game board. Overlay the chutes and ladders with your chosen materials, whether it's creating a rope ladder out of twine, creating chutes and ladders designs out of masking or duct tape, fashioning a chute from two two-by-fours, or using an actual slide or balance boards borrowed from your youth services department. The more interactive and creative you can get with the chutes and ladders, the more impact your game will have. Once you have determined your final layout, tape down the pieces of your game board. If you're using a Twister spinner, choose red, yellow, green, and blue construction paper to match the colors. If you are creating your own spinner online or by hand, set your color parameters and get creative.

How to Play

- Patrons become human game pieces and can start to play as soon as library staff are ready. Use the spinner to determine what color the patron moves to next. If the patron lands on a square or a chute, that player must move accordingly. To win the game, players have to get to the end.

Marketing

- Leave little cutout Pac-Men all over the library, advertising the event. The Pac-Men can lead to the room in which the event will be held or to the library's gaming collection. Alternatively, Pac-Men can be tearaways with information about the event that people can remove.

- International Games Day is a natural tie-in for life-sized gaming events. Bringing big board games to life will move your International Games Day program to the next level!

Variations by Age Groups

- *Millennials:* Millennials may be more drawn to an after-hours life-sized gaming event. Play on nostalgia and re-create beloved games from the 1980s and '90s, such as Mall Madness, Guess Who?, and Mouse Trap. If you choose to re-create Guess Who?, replace the characters with pop culture icons from the 1980s and '90s. Serve after-school snacks, ask people to dress in their best nostalgic fashion statements, and decorate with classic party décor, such as an inflatable air guitar, a boom box, and a totally rad neon color scheme.

⦿ DUNGEONS AND DRAGONS

Dungeons and Dragons is the quintessential example of a tabletop fantasy role-playing game (RPG). A role-playing game is one in which players assume the roles of characters in a fictional setting. Players act out the roles of the characters in the story line through decision-making skills and the rolling of dice. Outcomes can change based on the actions of players and the changing narrative of the story line.

Dungeons and Dragons, or D&D, has been popularized in mainstream media as a stereotypical nerd gaming activity, such as on the Netflix breakout hit show *Stranger Things*. Characters and settings are based in a fantasy world heavily influenced by the works of J. R. R. Tolkien. D&D is typically played as a campaign over a period of time with a group of players who control the actions of the characters based on dice rolls and storytelling. Special dice sets are used in place of the traditional six-sided dice to help determine the outcomes of the attempted maneuvers based on the character's abilities and strengths.

A Dungeon Master (DM) or Game Master (GM) narrates and moderates the story as it unfolds according to the actions of the players. The DM or GM also controls other characters in the story whom the main players meet. Each campaign usually consists of multiple sessions over which the adventure unfolds. This time requirement can often be a challenge because library program attendance by the same group of patrons is unpredictable.

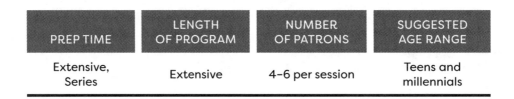

PREP TIME	LENGTH OF PROGRAM	NUMBER OF PATRONS	SUGGESTED AGE RANGE
Extensive, Series	Extensive	4–6 per session	Teens and millennials

Supplies/Shopping

- Module packs
- Dungeons and Dragons trade books
- Standard D&D dice set (seven-dice set)
- A tabletop board is not necessary, but it can help beginners visualize the landscape in early campaigns. Many modules and beginner books come with tabletop boards and prewritten campaign story lines to help new Dungeon Masters.

Activities

- Partner with a local comic or gaming store and ask for a demo of a campaign session. Many comic and gaming stores host D&D meetups; ask them to relocate to the library for a session. Invite potential players who have an interest in D&D but have never experienced a live session to observe and ask questions. Often, these meetup groups are part of official D&D Adventure Leagues, which are short, one-off adventures that are usually tied to the newest module. Libraries can become official Adventure League hosts, but doing so often takes time and has stipulations. Consider asking local games stores that already do Adventure Leagues to donate these short adventures, which provide pre-generated characters for one- to two-hour sessions as a way to ease interested newcomers into the world of D&D.

- Play D&D! As the librarian, or programmer, you will likely be the Dungeon Master. This role often requires a lot of preparation work to discover the narrative and framework of your setting as well as the characters involved in the campaign. Players can choose from among preplanned characters, choose names, and modify the characters to fit their personalities. Choose a short, introductory campaign to help ease players into learning how to role-play and become their character. This event could evolve into a larger, series program.

- Pair D&D with a *Stranger Things* program for ultimate millennial nostalgia impact. Have a marathon of *Stranger Things* episodes for patrons to enjoy and debate. Set up a D&D gaming area, pin an Eggo on a Demogorgon, and create buttons that advocate for your nerdom or D&D character: "We Love Barb," "Bards Do It Better," and "I Survived the Upside Down."

- Many teens may be intimidated by or unfamiliar with the concepts of Dungeons and Dragons and may need a tie-in program for that extra push. Have a nerd or board game night for teens with multiple gaming activities and include a station that showcases D&D. One of the biggest challenges is connecting D&D players to one another, and this event is a great way to introduce potential players as everyone learns to play together. International Games Day is also a great opportunity for teens to learn how to play D&D in a low-key environment that introduces players to basic concepts.

Crafts

- If you have a 3-D printer, create fantasy characters based on the players' characters or creatures they will encounter. If you're doing a series D&D program, offer to teach a 3-D design program so each player can customize a character. You can also scan people's heads with an Xbox One Kinect.

- Customize buttons for patrons to decorate with popular D&D sayings or to declare their character allegiance. Use bottle caps or put your library's button maker to good use and create keychains or magnets. Allow patrons to decorate their own buttons or provide preprinted D&D characters and popular phrases, such as "Lawful Good," "Sneak Attack," or "I Rolled a 1 and Survived."

Marketing

- Pair with a *Stranger Things* program or a fantasy-based gaming program. Adding D&D to this type of event will create a new element of nostalgia.

- International Tabletop Day is a timely way to introduce new players to D&D concepts.

- If you have partnerships with local gaming or comic shops, ask them to advertise your event or partner for a program.

- Create a book display promoting your program with fiction and nonfiction fantasy books. Expand the display by including *Stranger Things* books and read-alikes, complete with Christmas lights.

Variations by Age Groups

- *Tweens:* Although many tweens are more than capable of grasping the ideas behind D&D, it may be difficult to get them to commit to a regularly scheduled program. D&D can be a great outreach program during regularly scheduled school events, such as lunches or after-school programs where librarians have a captive audience.

▶ MAGIC: THE GATHERING

Magic: The Gathering is a fantasy card game that combines lore, strategy, and community. Your library may already be hosting Friday Night Magic events, but whether the Magic players in your community know about these events is a different story. By holding a library-led Magic program, you can not only create the opportunity for different groups of players in your area to find each other but also give interested but perhaps intimidated potential players a chance to see what it's all about in a familiar space.

Length of Program

2 hours (or as long as you want or have space and time for; also can be done as an ongoing series program)

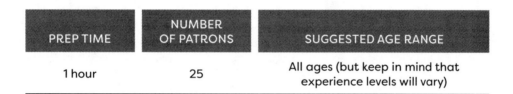

PREP TIME	NUMBER OF PATRONS	SUGGESTED AGE RANGE
1 hour	25	All ages (but keep in mind that experience levels will vary)

Supplies/Shopping

- Card packs or example decks
- Name tags
- Pens

Activities

- Because a lot of Magic groups gather at game stores and comic shops, reach out to those in your area and ask if any are interested in partnering with you on this program. Perhaps an employee of the shop would be willing to give an introduction to the game for attendees who are new to Magic.

- Because it's likely that people attending will have various levels of experience with the game, set up separate groupings of tables for different groups.

- In the room where you'll be having the program, be sure to set up some of your library's Magic player guides.

- For more information about Magic: The Gathering, visit the official website at http://magic.wizards.com/en.

PRO TIP

Don't forget name tags for everyone!

Marketing

- Distribute fliers to local comic and game shops.

- Set up a display of player guides (if your library has them) and include information about the program.

Variations by Age Groups

- The necessary variations for this program are for skill and experience levels rather than age. If experienced players show up, they'll likely want to jump in and get started playing; however, new and less experienced players will need an introduction.

OLD-SCHOOL VIDEO GAMES

Old game systems are returning, and retro controllers can now plug into computer USB ports. It's a great time to try an old-school video game program.

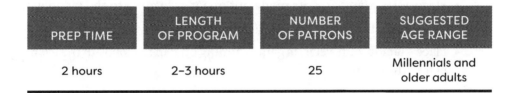

PREP TIME	LENGTH OF PROGRAM	NUMBER OF PATRONS	SUGGESTED AGE RANGE
2 hours	2–3 hours	25	Millennials and older adults

Supplies/Shopping

- Classic controllers for laptops, two per available laptop (inexpensive; try Amazon)

- Vintage video games for PCs (e.g., Pac-Man, Donkey Kong, BurgerTime, Pong, Space Invaders)

- Several laptops

- Video game systems owned by the library, such as Wii, with controllers, and games from the library collection (the original Mario is popular, and newer systems have classic games, too)

- Small prizes

- Nongreasy snacks, such as cookies or pretzels

Activities

- The most time will be spent getting and setting up the equipment for this event. As people come in, they can either sign up for stations or games (if there is a lot of interest) or simply start playing.

Crafts

- *Eat a Pac-Man:* Offer a station with big sugar cookies, knives, frosting, and decorating gels so people can make their own Pac-Men and Ms. Pac-Men.

Trivia and Other Free Games

- Have coloring sheets or video game history trivia sheets available for people who are waiting or not playing.

Marketing

- Place a Pac-Man and dots made out of paper leading to the video game section, with a sign about the event.

- Place a laptop with a classic game running on it in the lobby in the evening before the event.

- Ask local gaming stores and comic shops to put out fliers about the event.

Variations by Age Groups

- *All ages:* Offer games (e.g., Connect 4, Yahtzee, Mancala, Sorry!) on tables for people who are not playing a video game.

- *Multigenerational:* Offer an event in which tweens teach older adults or vice versa. Tween volunteers can play with seniors, or older adults can show younger family members how to play some classic games.

GRAPHIC GREATS

ALTHOUGH COMIC HERO FANS MAY also be graphic novel aficionados, the programming ideas for this theme focus on patrons who are passionate about series, anime, and comic books. "Japanese Cultural Night" will appeal to anime fans, and a "Vintage Comics" event will attract adult collectors especially. A focus on the women characters and creators of comic books makes "Women in Comics" a really good choice for a March event celebrating Women's History Month. Take an interest in graphic novels further by inspiring patrons with "Writing and Selling Comics and Graphic Novels" and a "Zine Workshop."

JAPANESE CULTURAL NIGHT

Japanese culture is multifaceted, fascinating, and alluring to people all over the world. Many teens (and people of all ages) are especially drawn to Japanese comics or graphic novels known as manga, which many libraries have in their collections. Capitalize on this popularity by offering a "Japanese Cultural Night" program, which can include hosting a manga drawing class and promoting interactive learning about the many different forms of Japanese culture. This program can be done even if you aren't an expert on Japanese culture or manga—just make sure to do your research!

PREP TIME	LENGTH OF PROGRAM	NUMBER OF PATRONS	SUGGESTED AGE RANGE
2 hours	2 hours	30	Teens

Supplies/Shopping

- Drawing pads or paper
- Pencils
- Variety of Japanese candy
- Chopsticks
- Origami paper
- Plates

Activities

- *Drawing Class:* If you have a talented staff member who knows how to draw manga art, ask whether she is interested in sharing her skills and teaching a class. Another alternative is to hire an artist to teach manga drawing for teens. It helps to have a large whiteboard and markers so the instructor can teach students on a larger scale. If you have access to an electronic drawing pad and projector, ask whether it would be of use to the instructor. Offer manga or drawing books for teens to draw inspiration from.

- The second part of the program can consist of learning about traditional Japanese cultural activities. Two interactive activities are learning how to properly use chopsticks and learning the art of folding origami paper.

- *Origami:* Teach teens how to fold origami paper into beautiful designs. Have talented teens help others and then display the creations around the library after the program. Discuss the traditional Japanese belief that one thousand origami cranes will bring good luck, and have teens create origami cranes. Origami cranes can also be donated to various organizations in support of cancer patients.
- *Using Chopsticks:* Teach the students how to properly hold and use chopsticks. Use the chopsticks to try to pick up the Japanese candy. Have the teens stack the candy and see how high they can balance it and how well they can hone their chopstick skills. After learning how to use chopsticks, the teens can taste individual candies and rate them on a scale of 1 to 10. There are many different types of Japanese candies to sample, so get adventurous!

Crafts

- *Paper Folding:* Create different origami designs from precut paper and instructions. Instructions for beginners can easily be found on the Internet.

Marketing

- Place fliers and posters promoting the program near your graphic novel or manga collections.

- Insert handouts with information about the program into popular manga series for teens to stumble upon when checking out the books.

Variations by Age Groups

- *Tweens:* Tweens can do most of this program but may need it pared down. It may be best to focus on one aspect of Japanese culture and an activity to go along with it. If you are working with tweens on origami, it helps to have other staff members to assist.

- *Millennials:* Many millennials grew up watching anime and reading manga. Many millennials are avid consumers of sushi, a traditional Japanese dish, and would benefit from a sushi-rolling class at the library. Check your library's food policy to make sure that participants can eat the dishes they learn to make.

- *Older adults:* Focusing on Japanese culture and its rich and unknown traditions is a popular way to draw adults to a Japanese cultural program. Offer an interactive element, such as learning how to use chopsticks properly or writing a few words in calligraphy.

⬟ VINTAGE COMICS

An exciting part of a comic convention is seeing all the comics and collectibles—both modern and vintage. Depending on the scope of your library's mini comic con, you can invite local collectors and shop operators who specialize in vintage comics to set up displays and even serve on a panel or two about collecting vintage comics.

Prep Time

Begin preparations several months before your event in order to book available presenters.

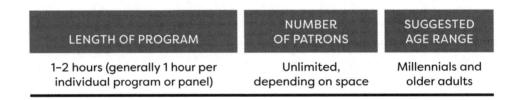

LENGTH OF PROGRAM	NUMBER OF PATRONS	SUGGESTED AGE RANGE
1–2 hours (generally 1 hour per individual program or panel)	Unlimited, depending on space	Millennials and older adults

Supplies/Shopping

You don't need a ton of supplies for this program, but make sure you have enough tables and chairs to accommodate the particular program you'll be putting on.

Activities

- The exact nature of the program(s) that you want to do relating to vintage comics is up to you. The event can be as simple as having a local comic collector set up a table and share his knowledge and collection with attendees or as formal as presenting a workshop in which a collector or comic shop proprietor talks about the nature of comic book collecting.

- If your event will take place close to the time when a big superhero movie is going to be released, you can tie in the collector or collection you're featuring with the movie (e.g., *The Avengers*, *Batman*, *Superman*).

- Regardless of how you choose to structure your program(s), be sure to leave time for a question-and-answer period!

Marketing

- If you'll be partnering with a comic shop for this program, you will have a great opportunity to partner in marketing the program, too.

- If you're doing a themed presentation or display, create a display of relevant graphic novels from your collection to promote the library.

Variations by Age Groups

- *Tweens and teens:* Although this program will likely appeal more to adults than to tweens and teens, that certainly doesn't mean that you won't have interested younger participants, particularly if a lot of vintage comics will be discussed and displayed. To keep younger participants engaged, create a fill-in-the-blank information sheet about the collection(s) that will be discussed or displayed (for example, "The rarest Batman comic is _____"). This handout will require additional collaboration with your presenter(s), of course, but it will be a lot of fun to put together, and your older participants might appreciate it, too!

WRITING AND SELLING COMICS AND GRAPHIC NOVELS

In addition to reading comics and graphic novels, many fans try their hands at creating their own. Drawing skills aren't necessary if one just wants to script comics, and the reverse is true if a person wants to be a comic artist. Whatever the case, a program that provides insight into publishing—whether on one's own or with a publisher—will be valuable to your patrons. Comic and graphic novel publishing is a different beast than prose publishing, and not many libraries offer publishing programs or workshops that are geared specifically to sequential art. The Internet offers a wealth of options for creating one's own webcomics, so this is a good opportunity to bring in one of your library's digital experts.

Prep Time

If you'll be hiring someone to lead the workshop, the sooner you start looking, the better.

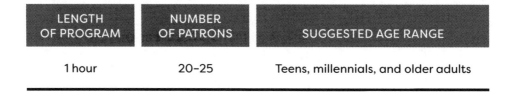

LENGTH OF PROGRAM	NUMBER OF PATRONS	SUGGESTED AGE RANGE
1 hour	20–25	Teens, millennials, and older adults

Supplies/Shopping

- Paper (optional)
- Pencils, colored pencils, pens (optional)
- Rulers (optional)

Activities

- A lot of today's comics—especially indie comics—are published online on platforms like Tumblr. When presenting a workshop about publishing comics, a good place to start might be the resources at hand, such as the Internet. For those seeking a more mainstream publishing opportunity, such as working for one of the Big Two publishers (DC and Marvel), an expert in the field will be the best option for presenting the necessary information.

Crafts

- *Make a Mini Comic:* If you're wary of offering a lecture without any additional activities, consider including a craft element, and encourage attendees to try their hands at making their own mini comics. The point of this exercise is to encourage expression as well as to display the accessibility of comics, no matter one's skill level.

Marketing

- Reach out to local comic book shops and bookstores and ask whether the proprietors are willing to distribute fliers for your program.

Variations by Age Groups

- *Tweens:* For a younger audience, the focus doesn't necessarily need to be on the ins and outs of publishing comics but, rather, on the ways in which attendees can go about making their own comics. Again, the focus here can be largely on the possibilities of getting one's webcomics started as well as on providing advice about how participants can keep their work and personal information safe if they're going to pursue a platform like Tumblr.

PRO TIP

Comic book shops and bookstores might have good suggestions about a person who can lead your workshop, if you're having trouble thinking of or finding someone.

⚙ WOMEN IN COMICS

Throughout its history, the comics industry has been a notorious boys' club—with male creators and characters taking center stage and their female counterparts generally falling by the wayside. Although it should be noted that women creators have always been present in the industry, this fact is being celebrated today more than ever. Further, in some instances, female superheroes have begun to outsell their male counterparts. A "Women in Comics" program is a great way to showcase and celebrate the contributions of women—the writers, colorists, inkers, and editors as well as the characters—who have propelled and continue to propel the comics industry. If you choose, this program can be combined or held in conjunction with a "Writing and Selling Comics and Graphic Novels" program.

PREP TIME	LENGTH OF PROGRAM	NUMBER OF PATRONS	SUGGESTED AGE RANGE
3 hours	1 hour	25	Teens, millennials, and older adults

Supplies/Shopping

- Paper (optional)
- Pencils, colored pencils, pens (optional)
- Rulers (optional)

Activities

- This program is a straightforward lecture that requires finding and hiring a speaker—possibly a comics historian or professional, or a local professor who specializes in this particular subset of comics and women's history.

Crafts

- *Make a Mini Comic:* If you're wary of offering a lecture without any additional activities, consider including a craft element, and encourage attendees to try their hands at making their own mini comics. In the spirit of women throughout the history of comics, have participants focus their comic on an influential woman in their lives (a relative, a teacher, a friend, etc.). The point of this exercise is to encourage expression as well as reflection on the importance of influential women.

Marketing

- Put together a display of graphic novels and comics written and illustrated by women as well as those featuring female superheroes and protagonists. Include information about the upcoming program.

- Reach out to local comic shops and bookstores and ask whether the proprietors are willing to distribute fliers for your program.

PRO TIP

Comic shop owners and booksellers might have good leads on a presenter or lecturer!

Variations by Age Groups

- This topic begs to be made into a series, because it is simply too rich to be covered in one sitting. Consider creating a book discussion miniseries in which several notable graphic novels written by women are read and discussed, with additional commentary about the creator(s). For tweens, works by Raina Telgemeier and Faith Erin Hicks as well as series such as Lumberjanes and Gotham Academy are great places to start. For teens, the writers and series just mentioned are still suitable, but you could also include Prez, *Persepolis,* and series featuring iconic characters such as Batgirl or Wonder Woman—both of which have had women writers at various points in their existence. For older audiences (and for teens), you could explore the popularity of graphic novels as a medium for memoir, such as those by Marjane Satrapi (*Persepolis*), Alison Bechdel (*Fun Home*), Lucy Knisley (*Relish*), Roz Chast (*Can't We Talk about Something More Pleasant?*), and others.

⚙ ZINE WORKSHOP

Zines have long been a source of self-expression and creative abandon. A zine is a small, usually handmade magazine that generally focuses on a particular topic—in some cases, a particular fandom or area of pop culture. The topic is completely up to the author, illustrator, or creator of the zine because the whole point of a zine is to express what one wants in whatever way one wants. The goal of this program is to introduce your patrons to zines and show participants how they can make their own zines at home. There are no hard-and-fast rules for making a zine, which is what's so great about them!

Prep Time

30 minutes setup + additional time for shopping if necessary

LENGTH OF PROGRAM	NUMBER OF PATRONS	SUGGESTED AGE RANGE
2+ hours (can also be a drop-in program)	Unlimited, depending on space and availability of supplies	All ages

Supplies/Shopping

- Paper (construction paper, colored printer paper, white printer paper in various sizes)
- Markers, crayons, colored pencils
- Scissors
- Old magazines or newspapers
- Glue
- Stickers or scrapbooking materials

Activities

- You can set up this program as a drop-in event or as a formal program with beginning and end times. The part that is going to require the most instruction will be folding the paper into a small booklet. If you design the program as a drop-in (or even if you don't), you can always provide pre-folded zines for patrons.

- The Wikibooks page "Zine Making/Putting Pages Together" (https://en.wiki books.org/wiki/Zine_Making/Putting_pages_together) has great examples of different sizes of zines you can make by doing different folds and cuts on various sizes of paper.
- Put out all your supplies and encourage patrons to get creative! Include example zines to help inspire participants.

Marketing

- Put together a display of paper craft and scrapbooking books and include information about the upcoming program. Include withdrawn magazines in the display, too!

- Put together a display of comics and graphic novels and include information about the upcoming program (emphasize using zines to make homemade comics).

Variations by Age Groups

- Younger zinesters might need additional help and guidance in assembling their zines.

- If you are planning to have a themed zine creation program, consider tailoring it to a specific age group. For example, you could focus on recipe zines for an older audience and zines all about a popular middle-grade book series for tweens.

HARRY POTTER: THE BOY WHO LIVED AND WILL NEVER DIE

FANS OF THE WIZARDING BOOKS, movies, and now screenplays are aging, but their love of the series continues. J. K. Rowling continues to offer new publications and material, which gives libraries more chances for celebratory parties. But who needs a reason? Consider offering a Harry Potter fandom event for fans who are . . . older than kids, around July 31, Harry's official birthday.

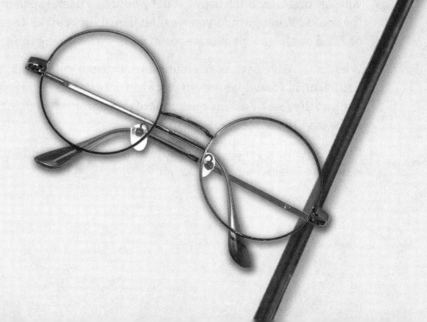

◉ BEYOND HARRY BOOK DISCUSSION

Harry Potter fans are passionate and always looking for new ways to enjoy their favorite stories. As new stories and movies are released, a trivia night and book discussion will appeal to these fans.

PREP TIME	LENGTH OF PROGRAM	NUMBER OF PATRONS	SUGGESTED AGE RANGE
2 hours	1 hour	35	Teens and millennials

Supplies/Shopping

- Sticky notes
- Pens
- Chess games (optional)

Activities

- *Vote on Favorites:* Ask participants to name their favorite scenes from each book. Take suggestions first, then vote on each book and then on overall favorites.

- *Enter Harry's World:* Invite everyone to fill out a sheet of questions about Harry's world. Questions can include the following: What subject would you do best in at Hogwarts and why? Which of Hagrid's beasts would you want as a pet? Which feasts would you like to attend? What position would you play on a Quidditch team? What would be a useful spell not covered by the books? Where would you wear an invisibility cloak? These sheets can be filled out in groups at tables or in pairs with sharing time.

- *Who Am I?:* Give each participant a sticky note with a character's name written on it. Participants then place the note on their forehead and figure out who they are by asking questions of those around them in this variation of the traditional ice breaker game.

- *Chess:* Offer time for chess as people come in or at the end while attendees watch the final scene of the last movie.

- *Acting Out Scenes:* Invite people to read short scenes from the favorites list aloud, taking parts.

- *Wizard Improv:* Offer improv scenarios and invite audience members to act them out—for example, Ron's father is offered a raise at his office, Hogwarts celebrates its twenty-fifth reunion, Hagrid goes on a date.

Costumes

- Invite participants to wear robes and other Harry Potter costume elements.

Trivia and Other Free Games

- Many websites have Harry Potter trivia questions. Call out questions periodically for fun between events.

Marketing

- Displays with chess pieces and some Harry Potter trivia questions on a handout will highlight this event.

Variations by Age Groups

- *Tweens or older adults:* Show one of the movies for tweens or for families along with trivia questions and voting on favorites.

◆ HARRY POTTER FOOD FEST— BUTTERBEER AND JELLY BEAN TASTING

Previously only a visual feast, Harry Potter's world of treats can be brought to your library. As tweens and teens, millennials were in awe and wonderment, just like Harry, as he discovered new sweets and snacks at Hogwarts and Hogsmeade. Bring Harry's world to life by experimenting with different recipes for butterbeer, bravely taste testing Bertie Bott's Every Flavour Beans, and more.

The scents and smells will transport readers back to when they first met Harry, Ron, and Hermione. The food and drink possibilities are nearly limitless in the Harry Potter universe, and these are just a few options. If you choose to serve alcoholic beverages, check with your library director and board before proceeding, and make sure everyone is 21 and over.

PREP TIME	LENGTH OF PROGRAM	NUMBER OF PATRONS	SUGGESTED AGE RANGE
3–4 hours	1–2 hours	30	Millennials

Supplies/Shopping

- Bertie Bott's Every Flavour Beans (available online)
- Bowls (large and small)
- Large spoons or ladles
- Microwave
- Plastic and Styrofoam cups
- Small plates
- Plastic spoons
- Wax paper
- Meltable chocolate or vanilla wafers
- Pretzel rods
- Decorating icing
- Variety of toppings
- Tea leaves
- Water
- Lollipops
- Pop Rocks
- Honey
- Small potion bottles with stoppers
- Glitter
- Food coloring
- Clear glue
- Corn syrup
- Markers
- Vinyl stickers or decals

BUTTERBEER INGREDIENTS (without alcohol) ————————————————

- Butterscotch topping
- Soda water
- Caramel sauce
- Cream soda (cans or bottles)
- Whipped cream

BUTTERBEER INGREDIENTS (with alcohol) ——————————————————

- Spiced rum
- Butterscotch Schnapps
- Imitation butter flavoring
- Chilled cream soda (cans or bottles)
- Vanilla or butterscotch ice cream

Activities

- *Reading the Leaves*: See into the future at Divination class and decipher tea leaves (hopefully better than Professor Trelawney). Brew some hot water and provide tea leaves for patrons to determine their future after drinking the tea. Print out common tea leaf markings and their interpretations (www. teausa.com/14531/reading-tea-leaves). Have patrons work in pairs to read each other's tea leaves and share funny ones with the group.

- *Edible Wands*: Participants can create their own edible Muggle wands using pretzel rods. Dip pretzels in melted chocolate and have patrons personalize each wand using icing and different toppings. Another dipping option is to provide melted vanilla or chocolate wafers in Hogwarts house colors: blue for Ravenclaw, red for Gryffindor, yellow for Hufflepuff, and green for Slytherin. Place the wands on wax paper to cool off for a few minutes before eating.

- *Acid Pops*: Sparks fly when attendees create Acid Pops! Heat up a small bowl of honey in the microwave for twenty seconds and coat the honey around a lollipop. Dip the lollipop into various flavors of Pop Rocks and let it cool.

- *Bean Tasting*: Ask patrons to rank the different flavors of Bertie Bott's Every Flavour Beans. Do this as a group activity if you have a whiteboard or chalkboard. Create scorecards if you are doing this as an individual activity, and separate a few of the flavors into small cups or plates for patrons to take as the program begins. Announce the most loved and hated flavors at the program and post online.

- *Butterbeer Bash:* Make butterbeer, the quintessential drink of the Three Broomsticks and essential for a Harry Potter food-tasting program. Butterbeer instructions can be found online (http://allrecipes.com/recipe/butterbeer-ii).
    1. Combine butterscotch topping (2 tbsp.) and soda water (1 c.) in a plastic cup; stir until thoroughly mixed. Add the cream soda (1 c.).
    2. Stir the whipped cream (2 tbsp.) and caramel sauce (2 tbsp.) together in a small bowl.
    3. Spoon onto the soda mixture. Stir lightly; it will froth.

- If your library allows alcohol consumption on-site, consider offering an alcoholic butterbeer, which is much more likely to draw the targeted millennial crowds. Alcoholic butterbeer instructions can be found online (http://allrecipes.com/recipe/240678/maters-adult-butterbeer).
    1. Stir spiced rum (1 oz.) and Butterscotch Schnapps (1 oz.) together in a plastic cup.
    2. Pour butter flavoring (½ tsp.) and one can of chilled cream soda into the cup.
    3. Add a small scoop of vanilla or butterscotch ice cream to the soda mixture.

Crafts

- *Potion Power:* Create popular potions such as Veritaserum, Felix Felicis, Amortentia, and Draught of Living Death. Although most potions are meant to be drunk, these are meant for decoration and personality. After all, who wouldn't like to have a little luck on hand at work? Provide small bottles and stoppers for patrons to take the potion of their choice home for luck, truth, love, and more. Fill bottles two-thirds full with hot water, then add equal parts clear glue and corn syrup until you feel it is the right consistency for your potion. Add color and flair with food dye and glitter. Patrons can personalize their bottles and label them with markers, vinyl stickers, or decals.

Trivia and Other Free Games

- Create a trivia game either on paper or digitally to identify the various potions and foods and the key roles each plays in the Harry Potter world. Ask how characters used the potions, what are the potions' identifying factors, and more.

- Hermione used logic to choose the correct potion in *Harry Potter and the Sorcerer's Stone* and helped Harry move on to the next challenge to save the Stone from Voldemort. Create a potion (or Harry Potter–themed) riddle that patrons must solve.

Marketing

- If your library has a café or vending machine, advertise in this area for hungry patrons to consider while they stop for a snack.

- Don't forget to advertise near J. K. Rowling's books, including her adult books, because many millennials may read outside the Harry Potter series.

- Create an interactive display of Bertie Bott's Every Flavour Beans and ask patrons to create their own disgusting flavor.

- Place all the beans in a covered jar at a public services desk. Patrons can guess how many beans are in the jar, and the winner receives a packet of Bertie Bott's!

Variations by Age Groups

- *Tweens and teens:* Create chocolate frogs in a candy frog mold, or create a mold using a 3-D printer if you have one. Melt chocolate wafers in the microwave and allow the chocolate to set in the mold.

- *All ages:* Both Dumbledore and Ron Weasley have claimed that they are most proud of being on a Chocolate Frog card. What would go on the back of your Chocolate Frog card? Templates can be printed out online. Use a green screen and props or a digital camera to go that extra mile and insert patrons' pictures on their Chocolate Frog cards.

HARRY POTTER WEARABLES AND MORE

So many good craft ideas and activities are available for this series that they could have their own program. If the library is offering a weeklong series of Harry Potter events, perhaps one session could be devoted to crafts. Staff need not be crafty to attempt many of these projects. A range of activities for different skill levels is provided.

PREP TIME	LENGTH OF PROGRAM	NUMBER OF PATRONS	SUGGESTED AGE RANGE
3 hours, including shopping	90 minutes to 2 hours	20	14+

Supplies/Shopping

COLORING

- Harry Potter coloring pages (free online to print, or purchase Harry Potter coloring book)
- Colored pencils

SCARVES

- Gold and maroon polar fleece (¼ yard of each color, cut into 4" × 18" strips)
- Threaded sewing machines, or maroon thread and needles for hand sewing
- Scissors (large and small)

QUOTE CRAFTS

- Iron-on transfer paper for ink-jet printers or photo fabric for ink-jet printers
- Tote bags (inexpensive, plain)
- Iron and ironing board
- Permanent markers (assorted colors)

STUFFED OWL PILLOW

- White, gray, and brown plain or patterned polar fleece for two pillows (½ yard of each color)
- White and black polar fleece for eyes (¼ yard of each color)
- Fabric glue
- 1 bag stuffing per two pillows
- Needles and thread or threaded sewing machines
- Large, sharp sewing scissors

DEATHLY HALLOWS PENDANT

- Beading craft wire, 20 gauge
- Wire cutters
- Long-nose pliers
- Jump rings (color to match wire)

Activities

- Choose at least three or four crafts for this event, along with the coloring station. Try making all the crafts before the program to test equipment.

- Set up tables with supplies for one craft on each table. Participants can choose what they would like to make, then move on to another table. Staff can demonstrate each craft before people begin.

- *Scarves:* Needles and thread for hand sewing or sewing machines are needed for the scarves, along with precut sections of fleece. Find very easy instructions for scarves at www.onmysideoftheroom.com/ easy-harry-potter-scarf-tutorial.

- *Quote Crafts:* Set up an ink-jet printer with the printable fabric near some of the books and a laptop so people can type and print some quotes. The ironing board with iron should be near this station. The tote bags can be decorated with permanent markers after the quotes are ironed on.

- *Stuffed Owl Pillow:* Many free templates for owl pillows are available online (e.g., www.craftideas.info/html/felt_owl_template_d.html). Print several copies of the stuffed owl pillow pattern and place near scissors and fleece at the station. Cover the table if fabric glue will be used, or set up sewing machines or equipment for hand sewing if preferred. Patrons may want to begin this craft at the beginning of the program so glue can dry before stuffing.

- *Deathly Hallows Pendant*: Wire, long-nose pliers, and wire cutters as well as pictures of the Deathly Hallows symbol make up the pendant craft station. Using the pliers and wire cutters, participants can bend and manipulate the wire into Deathly Hallows shapes. A jump ring can be affixed to the top of the shape, and crafters can then thread the pendants onto chains or necklaces they already own.

Costumes

- Patrons who wear any Harry Potter colors or gear to the program can receive a small prize.

- As participants enter, have them paint a lightning bolt on their forehead (use costume makeup or an eyebrow pencil, being sure to wipe off the pencil in between uses) and choose their house.

Marketing

- Have staff wear Harry Potter scarves for a week prior to the event, especially if registration is low.

- Create bookmarks with prominent lightning bolts and a list of Harry Potter activities or materials in the library and include program information.

- Display samples of the crafts near the best-selling book and media areas that have high traffic.

Variations by Age Groups

- *All ages—Butterbeer and Paint or Draw Night*: Provide small canvases, brushes, and oil paint sets to share. Participants can paint or draw an illustration or a cover from the books while watching one of the movies and enjoying butterbeer (for butterbeer instructions, see the "Harry Potter Food Fest" program description).

- *Older adults—Quote Scarf*: Patrons can print quotes from the books onto fabric and then sew lengths together by hand to form a scarf.

QUIDDITCH

Quidditch is a fiercely competitive sport in the Harry Potter canon and is featured throughout the book and movie series. Matches are played between two seven-player teams riding broomsticks, and the goal is to score more points than the opposing team before the game ends. Three Chasers use a ball called the Quaffle to score through large hoops on opposing sides of the pitch (three on each side). Two Beaters protect their teammates from balls called Bludgers, which are enchanted to attack players and prevent them from scoring. The game ends when the Seeker catches the Golden Snitch, a tiny enchanted ball that flies around the arena. The Golden Snitch is worth 150 points and often wins the game.

Unless you have magic broomsticks hidden at your library, Quidditch needs to be modified for the Muggle world. In 2005, Quidditch was brought to life at Middlebury College in Vermont. It evolved into intramural games, and in 2007 the first intercollegiate match was played. There is even an International Quidditch Association that is responsible for leadership of the sport throughout the world. For official rules, see the International Quidditch Association's website at www.iqaquidditch.org.

Quidditch is a cultural touchstone of the Harry Potter world and even has its own book, *Quidditch through the Ages,* written by J. K. Rowling. Libraries can adapt Quidditch to suit their programming space, whether indoors or out. The game can also be adapted from a contact sport to limited contact.

PRO TIP

Permission slips or waivers are a good idea because patrons will be running and there is a higher likelihood of injury than in a traditional library fandom program.

PREP TIME	LENGTH OF PROGRAM	NUMBER OF PATRONS	SUGGESTED AGE RANGE
3 hours	1 hour	14 per match, multiple matches allowed	Tweens and teens

Supplies/Shopping

- 6 hula hoops
- Gold spray paint or duct tape
- Rope or PVC pipe
- 4 foam balls (2 of the same color for Bludgers, 1 of a different color for the Quaffle, 1 of a different color for the Snitch)
- 14 brooms or pool noodles

Activities

- Prep the brooms or pool noodles to identify the different teams. Add duct tape stripes to four brooms, two of each color to identify the Beaters on each team. Pool noodles are a cheaper alternative to brooms and can be color coordinated for the different teams. You can also ask patrons to bring their own brooms to cut down on costs.

- Spray paint or duct tape the goal posts a few days before the event. Set up the goal posts on opposite sides of the pitch at alternating heights. If your program is indoors, hang the goal posts from the ceiling. Alternatively, you can attach the hula hoops to PVC pipes and create bases for freestanding goals.

- Create large scorecards to keep track of the matches.

- *Play Muggle Quidditch!* Make sure to group players of similar ages in the same matches.
    - *Rules:* One hand must be on the broomstick at all times, and the broom must be kept between a player's legs. No tackling or rough playing. Every player must play the role assigned—either Beater, Keeper, Chaser, or Seeker.
    - *Scoring:* Every time a Chaser puts the Quaffle through the opposing team's goal post, the team gets 10 points. The Snitch is a third foam ball of a different color thrown in near the end of play at the librarian's discretion and is worth 30 points. The catching of the Snitch ends the game.
    - *How to Play:* Traditionally, each Quidditch team consists of three Chasers, two Beaters, one Keeper, and one Seeker. If needed, modify your Quidditch teams to suit your library space and program. Chasers try to throw the Quaffle through the hoops; Beaters use the Bludgers to tag out Chasers and Seekers; Keepers guard the goals; and Seekers try to grab the Golden Snitch when it is tossed discretely into play by the librarian.
    - While the Chasers are trying to score, the Beaters try to stop them by throwing Bludgers at them. If any player is tagged with a Bludger, that player must stop moving for five seconds and drop whatever ball the player has in possession. If the Chaser drops the Quaffle, the other team can take possession.
    - The first Seeker to get the Snitch scores 30 points for that player's team, ending the game. There are two ways to win: either the team with the most points wins after the Snitch is caught, or the team that reaches 150 points first wins.

Costumes

- Muggle athletic clothes are preferred instead of traditional wizard wear so that players don't trip over capes and robes. Patrons can bring costumes for fun photos with friends at the beginning or end of the program.

Marketing

- Advertise Quidditch at local gyms, park districts, and community recreation centers.
- Use imagery from the Harry Potter movies and books.

Variations by Age Groups

- *All ages:* Is there a local chapter of a Quidditch league in your area? Check out usquidditch.org and ask whether league members would talk to your community and give a demonstration of Quidditch. If you can, host a game or ask a league player to referee your Quidditch tournament.

- *All ages:* Watch the documentary *Mudbloods,* which follows UCLA's underdog Quidditch team's journey to the fifth annual Quidditch World Cup.

- Don't have the space for Quidditch indoors or outside? Re-create Quidditch on a smaller scale with a tabletop version. Use varying sizes of craft hoops, dowel rods, bottles, and a Ping-Pong ball, along with plastic cups filled with butterbeer, to create a Quidditch arena. Set up ten cups in a pyramid on both ends of a table with the three gold-painted hoops attached to dowel rods and the bottles in the middle. Players must aim for the hoops and land the Ping-Pong ball in a cup on the opposite side. Players are allowed to swat at the ball with their hands, similar to Beaters. If your library allows alcohol consumption on-site, consider creating an alcoholic butterbeer for the millennials. Pair this program with the "Harry Potter Food Fest."

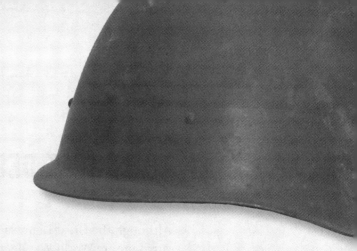

HISTORICAL ISN'T WHAT IT USED TO BE

DIFFERENT PERIODS IN HISTORY HOLD a lot of interest and offer a lot of ideas for programming. The 1910s, '20s, '30s, and '40s can inspire programs about making do during hard circumstances, a topic that is timely. Ideas and activities described in "The Great Depression and Wartime" program will feature those themes. The "Medieval Fest" will take patrons way back, and the "Victorian Charm" event will take them back—but not that far back! Plenty of activities for both of those programs will translate well for Valentine's Day or for reading programs. The Victorian activities also cross over with some steampunk events. The "Time Travel" program covers interest in time periods plus fantasy elements.

⏵ THE GREAT DEPRESSION AND WARTIME

Although the Great Depression era is hardly a fandom celebration, it and the surrounding World War decades can inspire a variety of programs covering a period that appeals to several age groups. The activities in this section are meant to cover a series of events, beginning with World War I and extending through the Depression and into World War II.

PREP TIME	LENGTH OF PROGRAM	NUMBER OF PATRONS	SUGGESTED AGE RANGE
4 hours	Several 1-hour programs	20 for crafts, more for speaker programs	Older adults (some activities are suitable for all ages)

Supplies/Shopping

SOUP KITCHEN

- Deli or restaurant soups (because of health codes, it will be necessary to keep these foods hot)
- Crackers
- Juice
- Bowls
- Spoons
- Napkins

LIBRARY VICTORY GARDEN

(volunteers or a local gardening club may help you obtain these supplies and organize the garden)

- Seeds
- Fertilizer
- Gardening tools

Activities

- *Skype Programs:* The WWI and WWII museums will set up educational talks through Skype on occasion. Contact them at https://www.theworldwar.org and www.nww2m.com.

- *Rosie and the Role of Women:* Invite a panel of professors, history reenactors, or other qualified speakers to discuss the role of women on the home front during WWII. It was during this era especially that women had to do the men's jobs as well as organize the needed food and supply drives.

- *Movies:* Host a series of movies set in or made between the 1910s and the 1940s.

- *Soup Kitchen:* Host a soup kitchen before a program on the history of gangsters, prohibition, and crime. Al Capone sponsored soup kitchens and used them for recruiting, tying these themes together. Serve soups, crackers, and juice before a history presentation by a speaker or an informational program put together by library staff.

- *Displays:* Put up a map showing where local WWI and WWII troops trained and served. Were troops from your area sent overseas? Did some fight in key overseas battles? Do any patrons have artifacts they are willing to lend for a locked display? A local historical society may have more information.

- *Library Victory Garden:* Organize a library garden that contributes to a food pantry. Do this as a partnership with a gardening group or church to get it started. Host gardening shifts for tweens, teens, and adults so people can learn about gardening in the climate-appropriate seasons.

- *Couponing versus Rationing:* Have a couponing speaker or local store employee offer cost-cutting tips. To contrast with this information, post rationing books and educate audiences about which foods were scarce during WWII. Serve Kraft macaroni and cheese, M&Ms (from after WWII), Spam, or dot candies to match the era.

- *Make It Do—Recipes and Foods:* Discuss foods and rationing from World War I through the Depression and into World War II. Serve apple pie, dot candies, or M&Ms to go with the latter two periods. Topics can highlight library cookbooks on those periods and cover dandelion salads, Depression Cake, One Egg Cake, Spam, and Kraft's mac and cheese.

Crafts

- *Knit Your Bit:* The National WWII Museum hosts a drive to knit items to be distributed at veterans hospitals (www.nww2m.com/category/knit-your -bit). This craft can also be done for local charities, after a short discussion on how people knit for soldiers. Have staff or a local knitting guild instruct a group. Supplies may be donated, or participants can pay a nominal fee to cover needles and yarn. This craft can be offered for different age groups.

- *Cards for Veterans:* Put out supplies and a few samples so patrons can make cards on a drop-in basis. Veterans hospitals or groups may appreciate cards made by patrons. A list of organizations that may enjoy the cards can be found at www.operationwearehere.com/IdeasforSoldiersCardsLetters.html.

Trivia and Other Free Games

- *Slogan Art:* Post photos from Norman Rockwell WWI paintings and other propaganda to see if patrons can guess the era or artist. This activity can also be done at other events as an ice breaker.

Marketing

- Advertise these events with patriotic displays and colors.

Variations by Age Groups

- *Tweens and teens—WPA Library Mural:* Designate an area for teens and tweens to design and paint in the style of a WPA mural over several sessions. An art teacher could be hired during the summer to coordinate this effort. The mural could also go up somewhere else in the community.

- *Millennials and older adults:* Canning is popular again and relevant to WWII especially. An informational program about how to can will likely appeal to these age groups.

- *All ages—Victory Tea:* Serve simple butter cookies, small sandwiches, tea, and juice at a Victory Tea while playing WWII-era music. It would be fun to hire a professional dancer to demonstrate dance steps of that time for everyone to try.

▶ MEDIEVAL FEST

Daring swordsmen, minstrels, turkey legs, and jesters are just a few pieces of the medieval experience that everyone learned about in school. Bring the Renaissance Faire to your library with activities that appeal to all ages in a jubilant atmosphere. Give patrons the opportunity to be immersed in the culture of medieval times with period fashion, entertainment, and crafts.

PREP TIME	LENGTH OF PROGRAM	NUMBER OF PATRONS	SUGGESTED AGE RANGE
4 hours	2–3 hours	20	All ages

Supplies/Shopping

- Floral wire
- Greenery on a wire
- Brightly colored flowers (real or fake)
- Ribbons
- Scissors
- Wire cutters
- Leather cords
- Beads
- Costumes
- Scarves or beanbags
- Puppet theater supplies
- Puppets

Activities

- *Sword Fighting:* Reach out to a sword fighters guild or fencing league in your community. Many colleges offer fencing as an intramural activity or sport; partner with your local college for a demonstration. People of all ages will be eager to see the clash of swords and touch the armor and weapons used by sword fighters.

- *Minstrel Performance:* Minstrels and bards made a living during the Middle Ages by singing songs, sharing news, and playing beautiful instruments, such as the lute and mandolin. Invite the local high school's orchestra to play and share their talents with the community.

- *Juggling Workshop:* Jesters were one of the many entertainers of medieval times and earned money by making people laugh and keeping audiences happy. Host a session for patrons to learn how to juggle. If you have a talented staff member, ask that person to help with the Medieval Fest and teach others to juggle using scarves or beanbags.

- *Food Fest*: Renaissance Faire food will always be a lure to patrons: turkey drumsticks, fried pickles, hot pies, and more. Food is not a necessity, but it will enhance the atmosphere.

- *Puppet Show*: Create a tween or teen StoryCorps group or workshop series to prepare a puppet show for patrons before the Medieval Fest. Storytelling and puppetry were art forms during medieval times. Work with tweens or teens to create and design the theater, make the puppets, and write the story in the weeks before the fest. There are many traditional medieval stories to use, but give participants the option to try their own humor and storytelling. Present the puppet show at the Medieval Fest with scheduled showtimes for audiences. This will be a multistage event: pre-festival programs, library programs, and a festival program.

Crafts

- *Flower Crowns*: Flower crowns were a fashion statement of medieval times (even before hipsters!) and can easily be created using fresh or fake flowers. Wrap the floral wire around a patron's head to establish the size of the crown. Use some light greenery to cover up any wire that's showing. Similarly, wrap flowers around the crown and add ribbons at the bottom for flair.

- *Leather Bracelets*: Design a leatherwork bracelet using beads and braids. Bracelets can be customized for any user, no matter what age or skill level. A simple braided leather bracelet is beautiful, and beads can be added to the design. The bracelet can be as intricate or as simple as library staff and patrons desire. Print out instructions to help guide patrons.

Costumes

- This is a great opportunity for patrons to wear Halloween or themed costumes in medieval traditions. Hold a costume contest or a parade to showcase knights, jesters, princesses, and more.

Marketing

- Get out of the Dark Ages and into the library with a Medieval Fest! Advertise activities for all ages, and promote the food, if applicable.

- Promote this program at your local college. Many millennials have a high interest in Renaissance Faires.

- Encourage staff to wear costumes to promote your program a week or two before the program and the day of.

⬡ TIME TRAVEL

Pop culture can't get enough of time travel stories. Whether it's the raucous fun of the Back to the Future trilogy or the emotional epic *Outlander,* fans prove their love for time travel stories time and time again. There are as many programming options for a time travel–themed program as there are different time travel stories. Feel free to stick to a specific story, explore the concept of time travel in general, or, as we outline here, send your patrons back in time!

PREP TIME	LENGTH OF PROGRAM	NUMBER OF PATRONS	SUGGESTED AGE RANGE
4+ hours (especially if you'll be writing your own trivia questions)	1½ hours	25	Millennials

Supplies/Shopping

TIME TURNER

- Crystal beads to make the hourglass
- Hoops in three sizes for the body of the necklace
- Jump rings
- Jewelry wire (28 gauge)
- Jewelry pliers

SCRUNCHIES

- Neon fabric
- Scissors
- Hair ties
- Needle and thread

FORTUNE TELLERS

- Scissors
- Markers
- Computer paper in a variety of colors

SNACKS

- Gushers, Fruit Roll-Ups, Fruit-by-the-Foot
- Goldfish crackers
- Capri Sun juice boxes

Activities

- Because this is a craft-heavy program, consider setting up stations for each craft so that people can move from one to another at their leisure.

- It doesn't need to be a focal point of the program, but consider having one of the Back to the Future movies playing in the room where your program is being held. Patrons can watch at their leisure while crafting and enjoying snacks.

- *Time Travel Faves:* Create a time line on a wall in your program space and ask people to pinpoint a time in history to which they would like to travel.

Crafts

- *Make a Time Turner!:* Fans of the Harry Potter series will be well acquainted with Time Turners, but even those not as familiar may want to make this simple and beautiful craft. There are many different sets of instructions online (see, for example, http://30minutecrafts.com/2014/07/harry-potter -time-turner-necklace.html).

- *Scrunchy Fun:* Send your patrons back into the not-so-distant past by creating simple scrunchies! Find scrunchie instructions at http://beautyblitz.com/ how-to-make-a-scrunchie#slide-5.

- *Fortune-Teller Tricks:* We all remember attempting to divine our futures during study hall, right? Many of your participants might not even need instructions for making fortune tellers—they made so many! Find fortune-teller instructions at www.instructables.com/id/How-to-Make-Paper-Fortune-Tellers.

Trivia and Other Free Games

- *Time Warp Trivia:* Ask questions focusing on particular decades.

- *Name That Decade:* Similar to Time Warp Trivia, ask participants to name the decade during which popular foods and fads were created or famous people rose to prominence.

Marketing

- Create a display using pictures of your library and community at different points in their history. Include on the display books that have to do with time travel, especially those that will feature prominently in your program, along with information about the program.

Variations by Age Groups

- *Tweens and teens:* These patrons may enjoy an '80s–'90s throwback program, too (though be prepared to feel *old*).

- You can tailor a "Time Travel" program to a specific time period or a book that's particularly popular (think *Outlander* for millennials and older adults and *Into the Dim* for tweens and teens).

◉ VICTORIAN CHARM

Although elements of this program on the Victorian era may incorporate parts of the steampunk theme, such as the tea, the ideas for this topic are more traditional. However, Victorian activities may be a good segue for those who are interested in learning more about the period and steampunk. The romantic and floral aspects of the crafts for this event are a natural fit for Valentine's Day.

PREP TIME	LENGTH OF PROGRAM	NUMBER OF PATRONS	SUGGESTED AGE RANGE
2 hours	90 minutes	25	Older adults

Supplies/Shopping

ROSEBUD POMANDERS

- Dried rosebuds (at least 25–30 rosebuds per person)
- Craft glue
- 2-inch Styrofoam balls (1 per person)
- ¼-inch ribbon to hang the pomanders (approximately 6 inches of ribbon per person)
- Straight sewing pins
- Scissors

TUSSIE MUSSIES

- Scrapbook card stock (12" × 12")
- Variety of small, lightweight trims
- Ribbon (several types up to ½-inch wide)
- Craft glue
- Scissors
- Flowers (real or fake; optional)
- Hole punch or stapler

VELVET CORD NECKLACES

- Lots of velvet cord necklaces (16–18 inches long)
- Cameo charms
- Jump rings (in metal color to match charms)
- Needle-nose pliers

Activities

- It is possible but time-consuming to gather resources for a presentation on the Victorian era. Consider having a speaker discuss fashions, crafts, and trends popular during Victorian times. Topics can include quilting, scrapbooking, jewelry and accessories, fashions, or weddings.

- Consider serving tea and butter cookies or small sandwiches during this program.

Crafts

- *Rosebud Pomanders:* Cover the entire surface of the Styrofoam balls in craft glue. Stick the dried rosebuds firmly into the Styrofoam until the ball is covered. Use a pin to stick a length of ribbon in the ball for hanging.

- *Tussie Mussies:* Cut a piece of scrapbook card stock diagonally to form two triangles. Roll each triangle into a cone and use the craft glue to seal the cone. Apply trim around the top edge, along with a ribbon for hanging (either staple on the ribbon or punch a hole or two and tie on the ribbon). Show patrons examples of elaborate, metal Victorian tussie mussies. If you wish, provide dried flowers to fill the cones. This website has good photos, though the directions and pattern are unnecessary: www.learn2grow.com/projects/floral/crafts/MakeTussieMussie.aspx.

- *Velvet Cord Necklaces:* Using pliers and jump rings, attach cameo charms to necklaces.

Trivia and Other Free Games

- *Meaning of Flowers:* Hand out information about the meaning of some flowers in Victorian times. Then show some bouquets or flower photos and have audience members try to figure out the meaning.

Marketing

- Hang samples of crafts around the library or display them in a case to help draw interest.

- Print information about the program on the back of the handout about the meaning of flowers and place the handouts at public services desks.

Variations by Age Groups

- *Millennials—Naughty Needlework Sampler:* Show some Victorian samplers and give participants a handout with examples of simple stitches. Invite people to sketch and then embroider or cross-stitch a rude message on a cross-stitch canvas or other fabric, suitable to add to a pillow or to frame.

HORROR AND THRILLERS

STEPHEN KING BOOKS ATTRACT TEENS through adults, and this program will tie interest in the books and movies to interactive fun, though perhaps without clowns! Active role-playing ideas appear in the "LARPing, Ninja Workouts, Self-Defense, and Fencing" events. Take it further with "Survival in the Wild," or survive with fantasy creatures in the "Zombies and the Walking Dead" program.

⚙ KILLER STEPHEN KING NIGHT

Adults do not have as many opportunities to enjoy Halloween parties, so a Stephen King–themed night may appeal. Teens just discovering Stephen King may especially enjoy this event. It also makes a good crossover with the "Zombies and the Walking Dead" program.

PREP TIME	LENGTH OF PROGRAM	NUMBER OF PATRONS	SUGGESTED AGE RANGE
3 hours	1 hour	25	Teens and millennials

Supplies/Shopping

- Syringe pens for prizes (optional)
- Write-on board and markers
- Small wooden cars or trains with paints (kits may be easiest)
- LEGOs (optional)
- Cheesecake pieces or mini cheesecakes
- Forks
- Small plates
- Napkins

BLOODY MARY INGREDIENTS

- Cups
- V8 vegetable juice
- Lemon juice
- Worcestershire sauce
- Tabasco sauce
- Horseradish

HAUNTED GINGERBREAD HOUSES

- Graham crackers
- Plastic knives
- Icing
- Red decorating gel tubes
- Small candies for decoration
- Small plates
- Gingerbread men and frosting and candy for decorations (optional)
- Plain cupcakes with frosting, Milano cookies, and gel or candy decorations (optional)

Activities

- *King Checkoff*: Provide a list of all of Stephen King's books under all names along with his short stories. People can check off ones they have read as they come in and eat cheesecake. (In many interviews King indicates that he has a slice of cheesecake before writing each day.) Who has read the most? Watched the most movies? Participants can vote on their favorite books and movies, then on favorite scenes. Best villains? Scariest scene? Biggest surprise? These questions should all lead to some lively discussion.

- *Alternate Scenes*: Have the group form five teams. Give each participant a sentence or a short scene from a Stephen King book. Each person adds a sentence and then passes the paper to the next person. After five turns, invite people to read their stories to their groups.

- *Pictionary with Characters or Scenes*: Divide the group into five teams. One member from each team selects a slip of paper with a Stephen King character or scene written on it. That person then draws the character or scene on a write-on board while team members guess who or what is being drawn. Teams earn points after the team guesses the answers within one minute.

- *Improv with Characters*: Give teams situations to act out that take King's characters into new situations—for example, a family spending their first night in the Overlook Hotel, a funeral at Pet Sematary, a delivery person at Annie Wilkes's cabin.

- *Quotes*: Pull quotes from books and short stories and have participants guess where the quotes are from. Also try this activity using movie clips.

- *Nonalcoholic Bloody Marys*: Demonstrate how to make a Bloody Mary and let participants sample the results, or have patrons make their own drinks. Many recipes are available online (e.g., www.food.com/recipe/non-alcoholic-bloody-mary-115915).

- *Haunted Gingerbread Houses*: Use graham crackers and icing to fashion haunted houses—or hotels. It is easiest to do this with small boxes, such as those for tea or Pop-Tarts. A pointed roof may be held up with icing and a little paper stuffed underneath. An option is to make and decorate dead body gingerbread men from "The Body." Or have patrons decorate cupcakes with half a Milano cookie stuck on top for a Pet Sematary grave.

Crafts

- *Trains and Automobiles:* Invite participants to paint small wooden trains or cars to represent Blaine the Mono from King's Dark Tower series or Christine. An alternate activity would be to design a possessed vehicle with LEGOs in five minutes for a mini contest. For the LEGO event, participants may take pictures of their creations but leave the LEGOs.

Costumes

- Advertise that people who come in *Carrie* prom attire will receive a small prize.

Trivia and Other Free Games

- Design a *Jeopardy!*-style game with such categories as characters, villains, short stories, Stephen King, and Stephen King's writing advice.

Marketing

- Invite patrons to write on sticky notes the King scene that they think is the scariest and then post the notes on a board near a display of the books and movies. Sticky notes shaped like hands or colored red would set the tone.

Variations by Age Groups

- *Ages 16+:* Offer a "Stephen King on Writing Short Horror" contest. Participants will write a scary scene in under one thousand words, set in a library or in King's fictional Castle Rock.

- *Crossover with "The Body" and* Stranger Things: Show the film *Stand by Me* and discuss similarities between the friends in the film and those in *Stranger Things* and "The Body."

LARPING, NINJA WORKOUTS, SELF-DEFENSE, AND FENCING

Live Action Role-Playing, or LARPing, takes the fun of attending a Renaissance Faire or other historical reenactment a step farther. Participants enter a game in character and in costume, ready to interact and build a story with a large crowd at a one-day or longer event. For this cross between theater and gaming, participants may need to learn realistic fight moves and other simulations. The library can provide information about local groups and show what some simple costumes and boffo weapons look like, but local LARP group representatives can better discuss the details of how to make costumes or how beginners can get involved. It is best to have a local LARP group representative lead your program audience through basic information with interactive scene acting. Find a map with locations at larpcraft.com. Advice for beginners, including dos and don'ts, can be found at http://geekandsundry.com/interview-mackenzie-jamieson-on-how-to-get-into-larping.

Invite a park district or gym representative to show silent, simple exercises, known as ninja workouts. Patrons may also enjoy basic self-defense movements that can be demonstrated by representatives from a local martial arts school. Sword fighters guild members or fencing instructors can put on demonstrations and discuss weapon history. If several professionals give short presentations over the course of a day, or each week in a month, patrons can use all the skills for LARPing or for their own personal education.

PREP TIME	LENGTH OF PROGRAM	NUMBER OF PATRONS	SUGGESTED AGE RANGE
2 hours (to contact speakers)	45 minutes to 1 hour for each of four sessions	30 each event	Teens and millennials

Supplies/Shopping

None

Activities

- *LARPing:* Ask the group representative who will be doing the demonstration to bring some props and examples of weapons as well as cards or handouts about the group itself. Ask about the room setup required and whether the speaker will need media projectors.

- *Ninja Workouts:* Ninja workouts are silent exercises that require no equipment. Ask a fitness professional to specify the space requirements and to provide handouts describing the exercises. Several websites have ninja workouts (e.g., http://darebee.com/workouts/ninja-workout.html).

- *Self-Defense Workshop:* Local martial artists or police personnel can provide a self-defense workshop. Martial arts studio operators often do workshops or demonstrations free or at low cost because they can promote their businesses while helping people learn some self-defense moves.

- *Sword Fighting Workshop:* Some sword fighters guilds offer educational workshops in which people wear period dress and discuss the history of swords. If such a group is not in your area, try staff at local colleges or history teachers and authors who may be able to bring some examples and discuss the basics of swords, weapons, or sword fighting. If any local organizations offer fencing lessons, those instructors may also help with the program.

Marketing

- Display fiction and nonfiction media and books on martial arts and sword fighting.

- Invite patrons to post favorite movie fight scenes or sword fights on an interactive sticky note board.

- Market the different sessions of this series separately. For example, tweens and up could be interested in sword fighting, while teens might be the best group for self-defense.

Variations by Age Groups

- *Tweens—Sword and Shield Maker Crafts:* Form groups of tweens to design and make swords from duct tape and cardboard, LEGOs, or even origami paper. Participants can make several types of weapons to take home. Participants can "test" their creations by lightly hitting the weapons against each other to see which hold. Then invite the tweens to make cardboard and duct tape shields. They can also draw the most spectacular shields for a mini challenge.

- *Older adults—Self-Defense Workshop:* Older adults may be self-conscious in a self-defense workshop or an exercise program that has many younger people also present. Offer separate sessions of those programs especially for this age group to encourage attendance.

◉ SURVIVAL IN THE WILD

End-of-the-world and dystopian novels have not lost traction since the popular Hunger Games book and movie series ended in 2015. Dystopian novels continue to dominate young adult literature and often feature a protagonist being thrust into a do-or-die, survival situation. Characters must survive based on their wits, knowledge of the land, and, if they're lucky, previous training. Help your teens learn how to stay alive and survive, even if thrown into the Hunger Games, by giving them firsthand experience with many of the skills Katniss and Peeta found helpful in the arena. May the odds be ever in your favor!

PREP TIME	LENGTH OF PROGRAM	NUMBER OF PATRONS	SUGGESTED AGE RANGE
3 hours	2 hours	20	Teens

Supplies/Shopping

ARCHERY

- Bow
- Arrows
- Targets

CAMPING

- Tents

POISON BERRIES

- Mixture of edible and nonedible plants and fruits (e.g., mushrooms, berries, garlic, mint leaves)
- Latex gloves

CAMOUFLAGE

- Finger paints (green, blue, brown)
- Cups
- Water

Activities

- *Archery:* One of the main skills any dystopian protagonist needs is the ability to hunt and live off the land. To do this, one needs to learn how to hunt for food or fend off enemies. Archery lessons can vastly improve a character's chance of survival. If possible, partner with an outdoor recreation organization or archery shop to provide archery lessons and target practice. Emphasize control and aim. This activity will most likely need to take place outdoors or in a gym. If your library doesn't have access to an outdoor area or open space, nerf or plastic archery sets with suction cups are available. Use a whiteboard or poster board target for an indoor session.

- *Camping:* Provide two disassembled tents for teens to assemble without instructions. Form teams and see which group can assemble a tent the fastest and most accurately. If a piece is missing or doesn't seem to fit the other pieces properly, ask teens how they would fix it in the wilderness.

- *Poison Berries:* Teens can discover edible fruits and berries and learn different tactics for surviving off the land. Bring in fruits and plants commonly found in nature, especially those found in your community. Ask teens to sort what they believe to be edible and nonedible based on sight alone. Take the next step and ask them to identify any of the plants or fruits. Create notecards to help teens match the vegetation and fruit. If your library is located near a community park or forest preserve, ask a ranger to speak about the different ways to identify poisonous fruits and plants in nature. Make sure patrons wear latex gloves when handling any of the fruit or vegetation in case of allergic reaction.

Crafts

- *Camouflage:* Is attendees' strategy in the Hunger Games based more on art than fighting? Never fear—they can still survive by learning how to camouflage themselves and blend into their surroundings. Have participants practice blending shades of green, blue, and brown on their hands and arms using finger paints. Bring in leaves and sticks for comparison.

Trivia and Other Free Games

- Create a PowerPoint presentation about survival training and tactics: how to survive a bear attack, the best places to seek shelter, how to treat an ankle injury or dehydration. Have the teens re-create some scenarios if applicable, then quiz them in teams at the end. Sneak in some Hunger Games trivia if you have avid fans. Offer a prize of a first aid kit to the winning team if you have the budget available!

Marketing

- Create a book display of dystopian books and tools that would be useful for survival. Place fliers in your dystopian books, especially the Hunger Games and other popular series, such as James Dashner's Maze Runner series.

- If you partner with a local outdoors or camping store, ask the operator to advertise the event in the store.

Variations by Age Groups

- *Tweens:* Invite local Boy or Girl Scout troops to participate and teach survival skills to other students. Set up stations for tweens to teach other tweens how to apply first aid, set up a fishing line, create a snare or rope trap, and more.

- *Older adults:* Many local community groups have disaster plans in place in case of emergencies. Organize an event for adults to learn about what an individual or a household would need to survive at home for thirty days and what your community's disaster plan is.

⏺ ZOMBIES AND THE WALKING DEAD

Zombies have had a large resurgence in pop culture in recent years largely due to the *Walking Dead* graphic novels and hit television show, and other hit books and movies have been given the zombie treatment as well. Zombies have never truly left the mainstream and are a cultural touchstone with all ages, thanks to George Romero's *Night of the Living Dead* and *World War Z* by Max Brooks. Hosting a zombie program at the library can encourage creativity among younger zombie fans and introduce new patrons to the variety of library programming and your graphic novel collection. Your zombie program can be as elaborate as you choose, given an unending amount of undead activities.

PREP TIME	LENGTH OF PROGRAM	NUMBER OF PATRONS	SUGGESTED AGE RANGE
3 hours	1–2 hours	20–25	Teens

Supplies/Shopping

ZOMBIE SURVIVAL GAME

(supplies can vary depending on what you can scrounge up)

- Backpack
- Matches
- Candle
- Flashlight
- Duct tape
- Screwdriver
- Water bottle
- Empty medicine bottle
- Can opener
- Hand mirror
- Radio
- Food can

ZOMBIE MAKEUP

- Zombie makeup kit (or use liquid latex, stage blood, paintbrushes, and a basic makeup kit)
- Paper towels
- Paper cups

ZOMBIE CRAFT

- Barbie or other small dolls
- Gray spray paint
- Dark color paints
- Paintbrushes

Activities

- *Zombie Survival Game:* Place all the supplies on a table in the middle of the room. Have the teens take turns getting one item from the table. Ask participants why they took each item and how it will help them survive a zombie apocalypse. Once all the items are gone, have teens reenact how they gruesomely died, with the supplies in hand.

- *Zombie Makeup:* Use a zombie makeup kit or ingredients to create flesh wounds on participants' hands and arms. Fill paper cups with water and encourage patrons to wipe their brushes clean when switching between ingredients. Before the program begins, make sure no one is allergic to any makeup ingredients, especially if you are using the liquid latex.

- *Zombie Prom:* Go big or go home with a Zombie Prom! Encourage teens to dress up in their best zombie formal wear for an undead night of dancing and fun at the library. Teens can come pre-zombified or learn how to become undead. Have a green screen background or photo booth for apocalypse pictures. Before dancing begins, teach teens how zombies would dance, or ask them to teach you! Throw in fun songs and remixes such as "The Monster Mash," "Thriller," and more. This program is a great after-hours event or lock-in theme. A library lock-in is a large-scale event that can combine many of these activities and crafts and will require multiple staff members. It is a memorable night that teens and staff will not soon forget.

Crafts

- *Zombie Barbie:* Turn ordinary dolls into terrifying zombies for a fun (and twisted) keepsake. A few days before the program, buy Barbie or other small dolls at a secondhand store and spray paint their bodies a pallid gray color. Teens can add more paint, rip clothing, remove limbs, and let their inner zombie rage. Undead dolls can also be used to storyboard and film stop-motion destructive zombie scenes.

Costumes

- Encourage the undead to arrive in costume! Give the costumes a twist by advertising a costume contest for the best zombified pop culture person or creature.

Trivia and Other Free Games

- Create zombie trivia from the Walking Dead series, *Zombieland,* and other popular young adult zombie fiction books and pop culture media. For example, show a screencap from a zombie movie and ask what movie it is from, or share a famous quote and ask who said it.

- *Pack a Go Bag!* If you had to leave your house in two minutes, what items would you take in a backpack? Would they be useful for survival or sentimental? How would you use the items to defend yourself against others and zombies? Have teens create a list of their top 10 items to bring, and ask them to share the list with the group.

Marketing

- The Office of Public Health Preparedness and Response at the Centers for Disease Control and Prevention created a campaign for the public about how to prepare for the (hopefully not) impending zombie apocalypse (www.cdc.gov/phpr/zombies.htm). Many posters and images are available for use by educators.

- A timely tie-in for any zombie program is Halloween. There is also a proliferation of sales on zombie makeup during this time.

- Create a zombie survival kit with Band-Aids, ointment, farewell notes, and a pen. Pass out these kits at outreach or school events to promote your zombie program.

Variations by Age Groups

- *Tweens:* Add a zombie theme to a generic library program for a twist, such as a Zombie Lock-In. Although most tweens may not be old enough to read or watch *The Walking Dead,* many are well versed in zombie culture. Many tweens can incorporate zombie scars and makeup using ready-made kits.

- *Millennials and older adults:* For millennials or older adults, consider offering a program about zombie folklore from other cultures as an interesting and educational experience. The undead often take different forms depending on their country and culture of origin. If your library offers themed movie trivia events, tailor a special one for zombies and the undead.

- *All ages:* Invite your patrons to come in their best zombie-wear to learn the choreography for Michael Jackson's iconic "Thriller" music video. Partner with a local dance studio or park district for this event. Remake the music video—change the scenery and choreography to suit your library and patrons. Encourage library staff to get involved; patrons will love to see staff members dancing side by side with them in the stacks. Don't forget to share the finished product on social media.

LITERALLY OLD SCHOOL

YOUR PATRONS CAN RELIVE PAST joys with these old-school events. Participants can experience the joy of the school book fair again and relive favorite book series with the "Book Fair" and "Book Fandoms" events. Attendees can experience a night of "Coloring and Preschool and Kid Book Favorites," get "Locked in the Library" for an evening of games, and meet other adult fans during the "My Little Pony" or "Pokémon" programs.

⚙ BOOK FAIR

The festival of books, posters, and other goodies that was the Book Fair was an elementary school nerd's dream come true—not to mention perhaps one of the first fandom celebrations. Why not take your patrons back in time by re-creating this special event in your library? In addition, it's a great way to spruce up your regular library book sale!

PREP TIME	NUMBER OF PATRONS	SUGGESTED AGE RANGE
5 hours	Unlimited, depending on space	All ages

Length of Program

2–3 hours (Because this program is a drop-in, you can have it last for however long you'd like!)

Supplies/Shopping

- Button maker(s) and button-making supplies
- Scrapbooking materials
- Scissors
- Card stock
- Tape and glue

Activities

- This program is designed to be a drop-in with various activities set up throughout the designated space. See the "Crafts" section for additional activity stations.

- *Book Giveaway:* If you don't have regular library book sales or are going to do this event separately from your regular book sale, you can opt for giving away the books rather than selling them. You can solicit giveaway copies from publishers or use withdrawn copies from your library's collection or advance reader copies.

Crafts

- *Button Making:* If your library has a button maker, this is a great chance to use it! The supplies for constructing the buttons are fairly inexpensive, and any number of stickers, old magazines, and even withdrawn books can be set out for patrons to cut up for their buttons.

- *Bookmark Making:* Like button making, bookmark making can easily be accomplished with scrapbooking materials, card stock, and some magazines.

- *Screen Printing Tote Bags:* This craft isn't as difficult as you may think! All you need is iron-on transfer paper, an ink-jet printer, and a laptop. Invite patrons to create their own iron-on designs, or have some ready to go.

Marketing

- Advertise this event in conjunction with your library's book sale, or advertise it at the book sale.

⏺ BOOK FANDOMS

Book fandom programs are a great way to reach dedicated book lovers in your community. Celebrate the release of a new book by a popular author, the next book in a series, or a book-based movie or TV show with a fandom party. Fans will be eager to connect with others and bond over characters, predict the future of the series, and compete in trivia and games to test their fandom knowledge. This template can be adapted and personalized for any book fandom that is gaining traction in your community.

PREP TIME	LENGTH OF PROGRAM	NUMBER OF PATRONS	SUGGESTED AGE RANGE
2 hours	1 hour	15–20	Teens

Supplies/Shopping

- Paper towels
- Temporary tattoo paper or temporary tattoo kit
- Printer
- Scissors
- Laptops or computers
- Green screen
- Camera

- Props
- Book giveaways and cover templates
- Card stock
- Bottle caps
- Craft resin
- Glue
- Magnets or bar pins

Activities

- *Speed Summary:* Have teens summarize the book in ninety seconds or less and explain how they fell in love with the fandom and why other people should read the book. This activity is a good ice breaker if many of the teens don't know each other and are shy. Have teens use these summaries and work together to create a book review for the library's website or social media. Introduce teens to the world of book blogging if they are unfamiliar.

- *Show Time:* Have participants re-create the book in ninety seconds or less using props or stop-motion animation. This activity can also be used as a book review tool.

Crafts

- *Fandom Tattoos:* Create fandom temporary tattoos with a do-it-yourself kit available at craft stores or tech up your program with a laptop, temporary tattoo paper, and an ink-jet printer. Use a design software product, and make sure the design is reversed before printing on the tattoo paper.

- *Candy Covers:* Re-create book covers using candy and different textures, such as blue card stock and marshmallows for John Green's *The Fault in Our Stars.* Digitally place patrons in the book covers that have humans by using a green screen background, or substitute dolls or stuffed animals.

- *Locker Magnets:* Teens can take home a piece of the program and declare their fandom favorites at school with locker magnets. Print out small, one-inch, circular fandom favorites of book covers, characters, and symbols that will fit into bottle caps. Glue small magnets on the backs and cover the images with craft resin.

Trivia and Other Free Games

- Book fans will appreciate any and all trivia from the book that drives them to compete against each other.

- Make bingo scorecards that correlate to characters, places, and events for the book or series.

Marketing

- Create a book display of the series, other books written by the author, or read-alikes to promote your event.

- Design fandom stickers that ask trivia questions and place them on book covers to advertise the event. To find out the answers, readers must come to the book fandom party!

- Promote your program with book faces for social media in which a user's face lines up perfectly with a face on the book's cover.

Variations by Age Groups

- All of these activities will depend on the age of the audience and the subject matter of the book fandoms and will need to be modified accordingly.

◐ COLORING AND PRESCHOOL AND KID BOOK FAVORITES

Everyone needs a break, so why not take your patrons back to a simpler time when the seeds of their fandoms were first sown? A preschool night for adults is a fun way for patrons to meet new people and share in nostalgic revelry.

PREP TIME	LENGTH OF PROGRAM	NUMBER OF PATRONS	SUGGESTED AGE RANGE
3 hours	1½ hours	25	Millennials and older adults

Supplies/Shopping

- Coloring books
- Markers, crayons, colored pencils
- Finger paint
- Large pad of white paper
- Playdough
- Shrinky Dinks
- LEGOs

Activities

- The most manageable format for this program is a drop-in with stations set up around the program space for various activities: finger paints, coloring, playdough, LEGOs, and Shrinky Dinks (you'll need access to an oven in order to make the Shrinky Dinks).

- *Storytime:* Everyone enjoys being read to. Provide some children's classics and ask participants if they'd like to read aloud, or the person running the program can read aloud.

Marketing

- Set up a display of children's books (including some classic favorites) in areas frequented by adults in your library (e.g., the adult fiction area, the reference area) and include information about the program.

Variations by Age Groups

- *Millennials and older adults:* If your library allows alcohol to be consumed on the premises, consider holding this program after hours and serving wine and beer.

- *Tweens and teens:* This program can be modified for tweens and teens, based on relevant nostalgia.

◉ LOCKED IN THE LIBRARY

Many book-loving adults would love to be locked in the library after hours for some peaceful reading! Although this event is not exactly peaceful, there are plenty of things for adults to enjoy. Offer a behind-the-scenes tour of the library, encourage talking above a whisper, and don't be afraid to let adults' fandom flags fly.

Theme your library lock-in! Many of the fandoms in this book can be made into a theme for your lock-in and can shape the events and snacks for the night. Potential themes include superheroes, Harry Potter, "Mystery Mayhem," game nights, and more.

PREP TIME	LENGTH OF PROGRAM	NUMBER OF PATRONS	SUGGESTED AGE RANGE
4 hours (shopping and setup time)	5–6 hours, after the library has closed	45–50	Millennials

Supplies/Shopping

MICROWAVE NACHOS

- Paper bowls
- Tortilla chips (assorted flavors)
- Shredded cheeses
- Olives
- Sour cream
- Beans
- Salsas

ICE CREAM OR YOGURT PARFAIT BAR

- Ice creams and yogurts (assorted flavors)
- Cups (clear plastic)
- Spoons
- Fruits
- Granola cereals

PRIZES

- Gift certificates from local businesses
- Movie tickets
- Vouchers for money off library fines
- Candy bars

Activities

- *Scary 'Brary:* Offer a scary tour of the library—show lock-in participants the basement or roof. Is there special equipment they could see? Or items beyond repair? Show participants things about the library that are interesting and memorable.

- *Library Olympics:* Create relays for teams of three to compete against each other—except the traditional sports events will be replaced with everyday library tasks. Sort books by authors' last names or call numbers on a cart, sort library due date cards by calendar year, and set up a book display. Time each team.

- *Video Game Tournament:* Choose several popular sports video games and sign up participants to compete. When one person is declared the champion in one sports video game, switch to another video game. Another option is to have multiple people compete on one platform, such as Mario Kart.

- *New to You Center:* Put out new materials, including magazines, and let participants look through them. Offer a screening of a new DVD movie.

- *Microwave Magic:* Invite participants into the staff lounge or a meeting room food prep area to enjoy microwaved nachos. Put out toppings, and allow participants to melt cheese in the microwave.

- *Chilly Buffet:* Assemble a buffet of yogurts or ice creams to put in clear plastic cups and layer with fruit or granola.

Crafts

- *Creative Accessories:* Use art supplies left over from other craft programs (or ask staff to bring in extra craft supplies) to make humorous vests or hats. Materials for this craft can include construction paper, duct tape, string, and yarn.

- *Try Out the Equipment:* As part of the library tour, highlight some of the crafting equipment owned by the library, such as a Silhouette machine, a 3Doodler, a 3-D printer, or simple die-cutting machines, and invite participants to try a simple project or design to take home. Also, pull out any equipment that patrons may not be aware they can check out, such as media kits, Chromebooks, telescopes, or other unique collection items.

Trivia and Other Free Games

- *True or False:* You can do that in the library? This true-or-false game is designed to let people know about library services in a fun way. For example, is it true or false that patrons can check out a staff member for an hour (if your library has a book-a-librarian service) or that it's legal to copy library CDs?

- *Library Scavenger Hunt:* Give participants a list of things to find or questions to answer throughout the library. Include donation plaques, artwork, displays, and other things. Patrons can work in teams. All teams should start with a different item in the list and go in order so they are not all looking for the same thing at the same time. Offer prizes for the most creative answers or the most wrong answers to increase the competitive edge.

Marketing

- A display with locks and chains will draw attention as will the words *after hours* in all print publicity. Participants will feel that the program is exclusive.

Variations by Age Groups

- *Tweens and teens:* Many of the activities for this event will transfer well for younger ages. A "New to You Center" or "Try Out the Equipment" activity can be swapped out for mini golf in the library. Create a mini golf course using weeded books as borders for each target. Karaoke or a lip sync battle will encourage tweens and teens to come out of their shell, socialize, and bond. This activity is easily done with a laptop and projector, or even just a laptop.

- *Older adults:* This age group may appreciate choosing among some of the activities without a lot of organized, competitive events. Rather than the "Creative Accessories" clothing craft, invite participants to create a bookmark from materials. Emphasize a night out, away from the kids, with downtime to read or view a movie or simply relax.

⬡ MY LITTLE PONY

Plenty of millennials will remember the original My Little Pony (MLP) TV series and accompanying merchandise line from their childhoods, and many of them are likely also fans of the newer My Little Pony: Friendship Is Magic series. Although your children's department may already have programs for the younger MLP fans, this program is intended to bring together adult fans and collectors of the MLP universe.

Prep Time

1–2 hours (If you're going to put out a call for collectors to be involved, you'll want to do so several months in advance of your planned program date.)

LENGTH OF PROGRAM	NUMBER OF PATRONS	SUGGESTED AGE RANGE
2 hours	25	Millennials and older adults

Supplies/Shopping

- Coloring books or pages
- Colored pencils, crayons

Activities

- *Collections on Display:* Provide tables for collectors to set up and display their collections. These collections can include figures, of course, as well as handmade fan crafts and fan art and any other (publicly displayable) MLP merchandise.

- *Collection Appraisal:* Invite an expert who can assess the value of a collection for those who would like to do so.

- *Collection Care:* Invite someone to talk about caring for collections.

Crafts

- *Coloring:* Coloring knows no age limit, so set out some MLP coloring pages and colored pencils or crayons as a passive element of the program.

Marketing

- Make sure that all your marketing clearly states the intended audience for this program because MLP appeals to patrons of all ages. Decide how exactly you want to structure your program and for what audience it is intended.

- Invite local comic and collectibles shops to be present at the fest, or, at the very least, ask the operators if they will distribute your fliers to their customers.

Variations by Age Groups

- *Tweens and teens:* This program may very well appeal to tween and teen fans of MLP, so there's no reason to discourage them from attending. As mentioned in the "Marketing" section, however, make sure that your marketing is clear about everything this program entails to avoid disappointing any younger attendees.

● POKÉMON

Pika-who? Pikachu! Pokémon began as a Japanese Nintendo video and card game in the 1990s in which players catch creatures, or Pokémon, with the goal of catching them all! The game underwent a major revival in 2016 with the creation of the augmented reality Pokémon Go app. People of all ages flocked to participate in the hunt for Pokémon at major landmarks and throughout public spaces. Libraries are often gyms or PokéStops for players and can use this momentum to capitalize on the Pokémon craze. Pokémon is a trend that is not going away anytime soon, and library staff should be prepared to help patrons evolve and share their love of Pokémon with fun, active programs.

PREP TIME	LENGTH OF PROGRAM	NUMBER OF PATRONS	SUGGESTED AGE RANGE
2 hours	1–2 hours	20–30	Tweens

Supplies/Shopping

- Perler beads
- Peg boards
- Iron
- Cardboard
- Magnets
- Glue
- Keychains
- Pokémon trading cards
- *Pokémon* DVD
- Pokémon character cutout
- Pokémon Bingo cards
- Bingo chips

Activities

- *Games:* Tweens can play a variety of games at your Pokémon event. Encourage them to bring their Pokémon trading cards but be sure to have some on hand so newcomers can learn how to play. Many tweens may have been at the tail end of the *Pokémon* television show or card games and could be unfamiliar with the original, analog version of the game.
  - ▸ Play an episode of the original *Pokémon* TV show and give tweens some background information about the evolution of the show. This activity also can be done during craft time.

- ▸ Create a real-life Pokémon gym or PokéStop for your program. Battle other trainers to catch a Pokémon of your choice with a life cutout that tweens must throw a PokéBall through. A PokéBall can be created using a red ball pit ball from a Human Hungry Hungry Hippos game (see the "Big Board Games" program description in the "Gotta Game!" section of this book) or borrowed from your youth services department (simply paint the red ball with white and black paint).
- ▸ Other fun games include Pin the Tail on the Pikachu and Pokémon Bingo.

- *Training Time:* Present some mental and physical exercises that tweens can do instead of virtual training to improve their personal reaction times and increase their basic strength.

Crafts

- *Perler Bead Pokémon:* A simple yet fun craft to personalize is Perler bead Pokémon. Pokémon Perler bead templates are easily found on the Internet. After forming the patterns and ironing, tweens can make their Pokémon into either a keychain or a magnet for their backpacks or lockers.

Costumes

- Encourage tweens to dress up like their favorite Pokémon or trainer. Show them different options for cosplay as different Pokémon trainers, even with their own hairstyles or a simple change of outfit they may have at home. Encourage creative forms of dress, and encourage tweens not to limit themselves to what is available in the app or card game.

Trivia and Other Free Games

- Create a Pokémon scavenger hunt throughout the library. Print and laminate Pokémon and hide them throughout the stacks. This is a great opportunity for patrons to explore different areas of the library that they may be unfamiliar with.

- Challenge tweens to a Pokémon trivia contest. Ask questions about the different values of certain Pokémon and what they evolve into, and show picture rounds of specific Pokémon for participants to identify. This activity can also be done as a passive program or contest.

PRO TIP

Sort out popular bead colors before the program, such as yellow for Pikachu and red, white, and black to make a PokéBall. When doing this craft, you may want to have multiple irons and additional staff members so a single person is not inundated with Perler bead requests.

Marketing

- Advertise near PokéStops and gyms, especially if your library is located close by.

- Drop lures near your PokéStop to draw in more people during the program.

- Offer a Pokémon program during International Games Day to attract new users and capitalize on a family or intergenerational program.

Variations by Age Groups

- *Millennials:* Many millennials grew up with the original *Pokémon* TV show and card game. Invite them to the library for a Pokémon nostalgia–based program. Screen an old-school *Pokémon* TV episode, trade Pokémon cards, and have special 1990s snacks.

- *All ages:* Pokémon is a phenomenon that spans multiple generations. Tweens, teens, and millennials grew up with Pokémon firsthand. Offer a program in which tweens and teens teach older adults about the various types of Pokémon and why it's such a meaningful game to them.

- *All ages:* Play an episode of the original *Pokémon* TV show and give participants some background information about the evolution of the show.

- *All ages:* Present an intergenerational program in which older community members (including Teen Advisory Board members) teach tweens and youth about Pokémon, its history, and how to play the card game.

SPORTS ARE FOR EVERYONE

SPORT FANDOMS ARE AMONG THE most passionate. Do the ones in your community realize how much the library can offer them? Tie sports, foods, trivia, and even crafts into popular big games with programs celebrating March Madness, the Super Bowl, WWE wrestling events, and the World Cup. The "Women in Sports" program is an inspiring session tying several sports together.

▶ MARCH MADNESS

Collegiate sports fans are often die-hards when it comes to March Madness, the annual springtime men's basketball tournament. This spring fever culminates in a month of basketball games and single-game eliminations. Bring together basketball fans to share insights about teams and players, fill out brackets, and kick off March Madness.

PREP TIME	LENGTH OF PROGRAM	NUMBER OF PATRONS	SUGGESTED AGE RANGE
1–2 hours	1 hour	20–30	Older adults

Supplies/Shopping

- Printed blank bracket sheets
- Laptop
- Pencils
- Basketball hoops game
- Plush basketball
- Gatorade
- Cupcakes or cookies
- Frostings and icings or decorating gels (in team colors)
- Cups
- Plates
- Napkins
- Rice
- Orange balloons
- Black Sharpie
- Funnel

Activities

- *Bracket Fill-In:* Invite patrons to fill out their brackets at the library as they debate and deliberate the best teams in the NCAA. Provide laptops or computers to do research on teams and players if needed.

- *Hoopla:* Play your own real-life bracket with friendly games of basketball. Have attendees sign in on a bracket and play using a door-hanger hoop or arcade hoops (these can also be used for life-sized gaming).

- *Insight from the Pros:* If a Big Ten school or a college is nearby, ask coaches or former players to speak. They can provide an insider's perspective on collegiate basketball that isn't often shared with the public.

Crafts

- *Team Colors:* Serve Gatorade and have patrons decorate cupcakes or cookies with their favorite team's logo, a favorite player's number, or basketball equipment.

- *Basketball Stress Ball:* NCAA tournaments are stressful; help patrons relax by making a basketball stress ball. Pour a little less than a cup of rice into a balloon using a funnel. Tie off the balloon. Stretch a second balloon over the first and cut off the tip. Use orange balloons and a black Sharpie to create a basketball stress ball, but any color will work for de-stressing!

Trivia and Other Free Games

- Many avid basketball fans pride themselves on remembering players' statistics and rosters from current and past seasons. Test that knowledge in a trivia challenge.

Marketing

- Promote your "March Madness" program at local sporting goods stores, gyms, and bars.

- Place fliers and posters on your sports nonfiction shelving.

- Create a display of popular basketball biographies and collegiate sports history materials.

Variations by Age Groups

- *Tweens:* If your library is located near a college that has a basketball team, ask the team to host or sponsor a basketball boot camp. Although this event would have to take place outside March Madness, it can introduce new fans to the game and get tweens of all ages active and energized about college sports.

- *Teens:* Create a literature-themed March Madness–style tournament using teen books or characters. Patrons can vote online or in person each week as the library gets to its final showdown. Brackets can be themed or broad.

▶ SUPER BOWL

Share the excitement for football's biggest event with a series of fun events and programs for adults.

PREP TIME	LENGTH OF PROGRAM	NUMBER OF PATRONS	SUGGESTED AGE RANGE
3 hours for some activities	90 minutes for most	35	Older adults

Supplies/Shopping

- Light snacks
- Drinks

BROWNIE DECORATING ─────────────────────────────

- Plain brownies
- Frostings in team colors
- Decorations
- Plastic knives
- Plates
- Napkins

Activities

- *Super Bowl Party with Pizza Tasting:* Show the game at an after-hours event with registration for adults. Offer a pizza tasting with pies from local restaurants and provide an opportunity to vote on favorites. Be sure to keep the pizza hot enough to meet health department guidelines.

- *Recipe Exchange:* Offer a favorite Super Bowl Party recipe exchange for patrons whereby they send in their favorites in the weeks before the Super Bowl. Post the entries online or hand them out in the library with information about upcoming related programs printed on the back. If many people enter, recipes can be collected and sold for $1, with the proceeds going to a local charity.

- *Vintage Snacks and Appetizers:* Cheez Whiz and Velveeta are two of the funniest and most popular food inventions of past decades. Discuss others, or ask a local food historian to review easy, beloved favorite snacks and appetizers. Foodtimeline.org has a list of brands that were invented in recent decades. Patrons can have a snack and take home a packet of recipes from this event.

- *Library Tailgate Party with Movie:* If possible, show a movie on a big screen in the parking lot outside the library. A football-themed movie would be fun, such as *Remember the Titans* or *Friday Night Lights.* Invite patrons to register for a car space, and allow them to tailgate at the event. The library can provide popcorn and water.

Crafts

- *Football Brownie Contest:* Purchase plain rectangular or round brownies and invite patrons to decorate the treats in their favorite team colors.

Costumes

- *Festive Fans:* Fans who come to a library event in the month before the Super Bowl dressed to support their favorite team get entered in a raffle for a prize.

Trivia and Other Free Games

- *History of the Super Bowl:* Teens and up may enjoy answering Super Bowl trivia. Links to trivia games about the Super Bowl can run on library Twitter feeds and other social media leading up to the event.

Marketing

- Display books set in the city where the Super Bowl will be held or the cities the teams are from. Travel materials for these areas are another option.

- Ask patrons to post their favorite ad or TV commercial from the game on a sticky-note wall.

Variations by Age Groups

- *Tweens and teens—LEGO Challenge:* Set up LEGOs in a maker area with a rough pattern so tweens and teens can build the stadium where the Super Bowl will be held.

- *All ages:* Have a pizza tasting for tweens, teens, or millennials in the weeks leading up to the Super Bowl with offerings from local restaurants. Restaurants may be willing to donate in exchange for advertising.

- *All ages—Super Food or Clothing Drive:* Have patrons place a canned or boxed food or clothing item in one of two containers decorated (use teen volunteers) for each team. The team that "collects" the most items wins.

◉ WOMEN IN SPORTS

Just as sports are not to be left out when discussing fandoms, women are certainly not to be left out when discussing sports. You can take many routes when planning a program that celebrates women in sports. For example, you can focus on a particular sport or athlete, but the program outlined here is intended to celebrate women's past and present contributions to the world of sports in general. This program could be part of a Women's History Month series. (For clarification, this program is not intended solely for girls and women!)

PREP TIME	LENGTH OF PROGRAM	NUMBER OF PATRONS	SUGGESTED AGE RANGE
2 hours	1½–2 hours	20	Tweens and teens

Supplies/Shopping

- Card stock
- Markers, crayons, colored pencils
- Scissors

Activities

- *Mentoring:* Invite a local sports team (high school, college, pro) to mentor younger attendees for an afternoon. The mentorship doesn't have to be strictly specific to the sport but can focus on team building and sportsmanship while touching on basic skills and fundamentals of the sport.

- *History Presentation:* If possible, invite a local female coach or sports medicine professor (or history professor, even) to speak to younger attendees about the history of women in sports, perhaps paying specific attention to groundbreaking women.

Crafts

- *Sports Trading Cards:* Have attendees create their own sports trading card. They can draw a picture of themselves on the front (or decorate the card however they want if they'd prefer) and write their stats on the back. The stats don't have to be sports specific—they can write whatever they want to share about themselves!

Costumes

- Invite attendees to wear their favorite sports team jersey, T-shirt, or the like.

Marketing

- Create a display of fiction and nonfiction books that focus on female athletes, and include information on the display about the program.

Variations by Age Groups

- *Millennials and older adults:* Show a classic film such as *A League of Their Own* and pair it with a discussion or informational session led by a speaker who is well versed in the subject matter of the movie (plan to extend the program time to accommodate this activity).

⚽ WORLD CUP

The popularity of soccer is growing everywhere! Catch the wave of patron interest with fun events.

PREP TIME	LENGTH OF PROGRAM	NUMBER OF PATRONS	SUGGESTED AGE RANGE
2 hours	90 minutes or length of game	25	Tweens, teens, and millennials

Supplies/Shopping

- Light snacks
- Drinks
- History of World Cup DVD
- Recent FIFA video game for library system, at least for two stations

SOCCER CUPCAKES

- Oreo Thins
- Plain vanilla or chocolate frosted cupcakes
- Vanilla or chocolate frosting
- Brown or black decorating gel tubes
- Plastic knives
- Plates
- Napkins

Activities

- *Game Time:* Watching a game on a big screen with other fans makes the game even more fun. While the game is on, teens can enjoy light snacks, play FIFA on gaming systems, and decorate a cupcake.

- *History DVD:* If it is not practical to show the game in real time, present a DVD of World Cup history.

- *FIFA Tournaments:* FIFA video games can be run as a tournament in which teens sign up and are assigned stations as they come in, but it may be just as rewarding for them simply to play the game while a real-life soccer game is on the big screen.

- *Meet the Players:* If any professional or semi-pro soccer teams are nearby, invite the players to this event for a meet-and-greet along with a signing. The players may be interested in playing FIFA with the teens or talking about how they got involved in the sport.

Crafts

- *Cupcakes with Oreo Thins:* Because these cookies are the right shape to look like the patches on a soccer ball, participants can make soccer ball designs on frosted cupcakes using the Oreo Thins and decorating gels.

Costumes

- Offer prizes for wearing World Cup gear or jerseys to the event.

Trivia and Other Free Games

- Create a handout with questions or ask questions at the event about game history for a chance to win a jersey, a book about the World Cup, or a FIFA video game.

Marketing

- Post a map with flags for the teams. Offer voting for favorites.

- Make a display with books by authors from the countries in the finals or books set in those countries.

- Create a handout listing library materials useful for learning the languages of the playing countries.

Variations by Age Groups

- *All ages—Book Goals:* People choose a country as a favorite to win and post their book reading goals in the month before the World Cup. Patrons record the title and author of what they read, and the library has a graphic to keep track of which countries are "making book goals."

- *Millennials and older adults:* Have a tasting event with food or wine from participating countries.

- *All ages—Semi-Pro Game:* Organize a bus trip for patrons to attend a semi-pro or college soccer game.

WWE

WWE fans may be on the younger end of the spectrum of fandoms, but they are no less passionate. They will be pleasantly surprised to find other fans at the library through some of these activities.

PREP TIME	LENGTH OF PROGRAM	NUMBER OF PATRONS	SUGGESTED AGE RANGE
1 hour	2 hours	20	12–18

Supplies/Shopping

- Light snacks
- Plates
- Napkins
- Candy bars (for prizes; optional)

ACTION FIGURE KEYCHAINS

- Eye screws
- Lighter (or Dremel with a very narrow bit)
- Keychain hardware
- Jump rings
- Long- and short-nose pliers

Activities

- *WWE 2k16 Tournament:* This WWE video game takes players through classic battles. Have the game available on a couple of platforms for casual play during the event.

- *Classic WWE Fight DVDs:* Have these DVDs running in the background.

- *LARPing:* People from a professional LARPing group can show some fake fighting moves for audience members.

- *Fight Fiction:* In the weeks prior to the event, invite people to describe (in 250 words or less) the best fight move that they could imagine ever being performed.

- *Wrestler Fan Art:* Invite wrestling fans to draw their favorite costume or scene from wrestling to post to advertise the program or display at the program.

Crafts

- *Action Figure Keychains:* This craft is described for necklaces in the "Action Figures Assemble" program in this guide. Again, this craft requires some adult help. In the weeks before the event, ask staff and friends to donate their mini wrestling action figures. Figures larger than three inches may not work for this craft. For tiny figures, use jump rings. Other action figures will work also because it may be hard to find enough small wrestlers. Heat the eye screw and then screw it into the head of the plastic figure (or use the Dremel to drill a tiny hole). Use the jump rings to attach the figure to a keychain.

Trivia and Other Free Games

- *Name the Wrestler:* Match the unusual name to the wrestler who uses it.

Marketing

- Place the action figures on a display of materials about or by wrestlers. Some materials may be for adults only.

Variations by Age Groups

- *All ages—Self-Defense Moves:* Have different sessions of self-defense training for all ages, but in particular offer one after the wrestling event so participants can see some real moves and how they should work.

STEAMPUNK IT UP

A COMBINATION OF VICTORIAN OR Edwardian period elements and gadgets makes this genre fun for all ages. Although the term may be new to some patrons, fans of steampunk are loyal and passionate. Many libraries are offering steampunk festivals, with costume contests, parties, discussions of books, displays of art or gadgets, and more. You don't have to understand everything about steampunk to enjoy it. Try out one of the four steampunk programs described in this section to gauge patron interest: engage patrons in "Creating Steampunk Outfits," challenge attendees with a "Ship Design Contest," throw a "Tea Party," or make "Timely Jewelry."

⏯ CREATING STEAMPUNK OUTFITS

The costume is often the most daunting aspect for people who are new to participating in steampunk events. This program is meant to give a brief history of Victorian and Edwardian dress, but more importantly, it is about the basics of putting a steampunk outfit together. Although this can be done with a slide show and movie clips, it is best done with samples of clothing. This event will require asking employees from local fabric, vintage, or thrift stores to bring samples or having a cosplay expert or theater teacher participate. Consider offering this program before the jewelry workshop or after the tea.

PREP TIME	LENGTH OF PROGRAM	NUMBER OF PATRONS	SUGGESTED AGE RANGE
2 hours	45 minutes	50	14+

Supplies/Shopping

None needed

Activities

- *Outfits on Film:* Show clips and images from steampunk movies that feature the outfits close up. Try *Hugo, The City of Lost Children, 20,000 Leagues under the Sea* (older versions), *Wild Wild West, Atlantis: The Lost Empire, Steamboy,* and *The Adventures of Baron Munchausen.*

- *Outfits Online:* Project images of steampunk costumes found online. Pinterest has many. Sewing pattern companies have patterns for full costumes. Online costume vendors have entire costumes available for purchase. Showing some of those resources will help audience members who want to get the whole outfit at once. The following sites provide examples of outfits for beginners to put together:
    - ▸ *Steaming Apparel:* Resources for Steampunk Costuming (http://steampunk.cnbeyer.com/starting.shtml).
    - ▸ *Adrienne Kress:* So You Want to Dress Steampunk (http://ididnt choosethis.blogspot.com/2012/11/so-you-want-to-dress-steampunk .html).

- *Outfits Piece by Piece:* Discuss elements of the costumes after giving an overview of what period buttons and shoes would look like. Each element will require some projected photos for audience members. Provide a handout with resources, books, and movies listed for further information. Blouses, jackets, skirts (over and under), vests, shirts, and pants should be covered.

- *Outfits in Detail:* Accessories are among the most fun parts of steampunk outfits. Show photos of hats, highlighting what types will work; goggles; belts; and military-style decorations, including chains. The following resource shows some easy accessories:
  - ▸ *Rebels Market:* 5 Easy Steampunk Do-It-Yourself Projects (www.rebels market.com/blog/posts/5-easy-steampunk-do-it-yourself-projects).

- *Outfits in Person:* Invite professors from local college theater, fashion, or history departments to discuss costumes. Thrift or vintage store staff may be another good resource.

- *Outfits on Parade:* Discuss local steampunk events and societies for which audience members could wear costumes and what types of activities would be appropriate.

Trivia and Other Free Games

- *Guess the Gadget:* Show types of steampunk weapons and see if audience members can guess what was used to make them. Reference the sites listed earlier or other photos.

Marketing

- If possible, hang up parts of steampunk costumes in the library to attract attention.

- Make a foam board cutout of a steampunk costume with a hole for the head so people can put their face through and take pictures.

Variations by Age Groups

- *Teens, millennials, and older adults:* A simple way to teach patrons about making costumes is to offer a parade with a tea afterward. Invite participants who come in costume to stand up and discuss how they put their costumes together. Often people like to share tips and show off projects, so it will likely be easy to get enthusiasts to share.

- *Teens, millennials, and older adults:* Present a program at a local thrift store and ask personnel at the shop to briefly highlight some tops and pants that may work. Participants can then try on different pieces of clothing and purchase their own outfits right on the site.

- *All ages:* Offer a photo booth with steampunk costume elements for patrons to try on. Borrow outfit pieces from theater departments or steampunk cosplay enthusiasts. This activity can also be done with a green screen and a London setting.

- *All ages:* Show one of the movies listed in the "Outfits on Film" activity in its entirety. Host a discussion of costume elements after the movie.

◈ SHIP DESIGN CONTEST

An imaginary airship design contest is a fun and easy way to introduce steampunk to new fans or to engage devoted ones. This contest could be popular when other steampunk events are occurring or when a few steampunk movies are being shown.

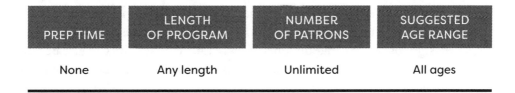

PREP TIME	LENGTH OF PROGRAM	NUMBER OF PATRONS	SUGGESTED AGE RANGE
None	Any length	Unlimited	All ages

Supplies/Shopping

- Prizes for winners (Include different age groups as well as digital and print entries.)

Activities

- Make print and online contest entry forms and specify contest rules, such as size of paper or entry and digital entry qualifications (no Photoshop).

- Invite staff from different departments or members of the board to judge. If there is an active local steampunk group, members may enjoy judging as well. Present awards for most imaginative, best use of ____ , and other categories to allow as many winners as possible.

Crafts

- *Draw-In:* Invite patrons to watch a steampunk movie while drawing fanciful creations and looking at books with ships in them.

Trivia and Other Free Games

- *Air Power Time Line:* Photocopy pictures or drawings of aircraft from different periods and invite participants to put them in chronological order.

Marketing

- Display steampunk books and art or modeling books to help garner interest in the contest.

- Hang up models of planes or airships above a display or in a high-traffic area to catch attention.

Variations by Age Groups

- *Tweens and teens—Make an Airship:* Provide paper of various colors and sizes, glue, straws, balloons, and other building materials for participants to design their own three-dimensional aircraft. This activity can also be done in a much simpler style as a paper airplane contest. See who can make the longest-flying paper airplane.

- *Millennials and older adults—Make a Model Airship:* Invite participants to make a three-dimensional airship model as part of the contest. You can specify building materials or simply invite people to bring in an airship made from anything, including LEGOs, that will fit into a library display case.

⚙ TEA PARTY

Tea parties in a library setting do not need to be expensive and ultra fancy to be fun for participants. Inviting people to wear costumes and serving fun snacks is a recipe for a successful event.

PREP TIME	LENGTH OF PROGRAM	NUMBER OF PATRONS	SUGGESTED AGE RANGE
2 hours	45 minutes	35	11+ (all ages)

Supplies/Shopping

- Chutney or marmalade
- Small biscuits or rolls
- Herbal fruit teas, or rose petal tea
- Teapots or electric pots for heating water
- Lemons (for lemon water)
- Pitcher
- Small butter cookies
- Cheeses (precut in squares for a tray is easiest)
- Fruit such as strawberries or grapes for easy serving
- Lace fabric or netting for tablecloths or other inexpensive coverings
- Silverware
- Plates
- Cups (for hot or cold)
- Tea party–themed items for prizes (optional)

Activities

- Set up tables with tablecloths. Although at most tea parties the tables have drinks and food available for self-service, it is easier to have a buffet-style event in a library setting. This way the hot water pots can be near electricity. People should get their tea and food as they arrive.

- *Tea Party Attire:* When everyone is seated, invite those in costume to stand and receive a prize or discuss their costumes.

- *Victorian Teatime:* Discuss the food choices and other foods that may have been popular during Victorian times.

Trivia and Other Free Games

- *Tea ID:* Print photos of foods or offer flavors of jellies and spreads and see if people can guess what they are.

- *Recipe Mania:* List ingredients of recipes that are true and false and see if patrons can identify either what the recipes make or which recipes are false.

Marketing

- Food events are usually popular in libraries, and handing out a recipe for a simple cookie with the information about the program on the back in the weeks before the event should add appeal.

Variations by Age Groups

- *Tweens and teens—Mad Hatter's Tea Party:* Show an Alice in Wonderland movie, followed by a Mad Hatter's Tea Party. Heart-shaped cookies or candies would be a fun addition to the fare. Invite participants to wear hats, and offer prizes for those who do. Show participants how to make a simple fascinator out of hair combs, feathers, ribbons, and glue.

- *Older adults:* Add a recipe exchange element to the program by inviting people to bring copies of favorite recipes. Provide simple photo albums along with scrapbook papers and stickers so patrons can make mini recipe scrapbooks with the recipes they receive in the exchange.

⚙ TIMELY JEWELRY

Simple steampunk jewelry can be made with findings and easily found elements such as chains, buttons, keys, gears, or watch faces. Because of the popularity of the steampunk style, inexpensive lots of gear parts or watch faces can be found at craft stores or through online sites such as Amazon for a fun group craft program.

PREP TIME	LENGTH OF PROGRAM	NUMBER OF PATRONS	SUGGESTED AGE RANGE
2 hours, including shopping	1 hour	20	16–30

Supplies/Shopping

- Charms (at least 5–7 per participant): keys, gears, chains, watches, buttons
- 20 necklace chains with closures (available at craft stores or on Amazon)
- T-pins, eye pins in 2-inch lengths (The antique brass color on findings is popular with the steampunk style.)
- Earrings (40 of each): wires, plastic backings, T-pins, eye pins (shorter lengths of pins will work for earrings)
- Jump rings in assorted sizes for both necklaces and earrings
- Craft glue that works with metal (optional)
- At least 5 sets of wire cutters, long- and short-nose pliers
- Faceted beads (assorted colors, including metallic, black, and purple; purchase by strand or lot at craft stores or online)
- Paper bowls

Activities

- Set up five tables, with four chairs and one set of tools at each. Place a necklace chain at each seat. Put beads sorted by color in paper bowls at a main table. Lay out T-pins and eye pins for easy selection.

- Demonstrate how to attach charms to a necklace chain with jump rings. Demonstrate how to add beads to pins and attach those to the jump rings and chains. Show how those same selection styles can be incorporated into earrings. If needed, project tutorials on simple earring wire attachment from online sources. Participants can also glue on buttons or glue small beads onto charms for added layering.

Costumes

- Show examples of steampunk jewelry from magazines or project online sources, and discuss how they are worn with costumes at cosplay events. If the jewelry class is part of a larger festival, offer a small prize for participants who wear jewelry made in class to other events.

Trivia and Other Free Games

- Show photos of goggles, fascinators, shoes, hats, unusual timepieces, and bags in the steampunk styles and have participants guess what the items are and what they are used for. To inspire future projects, discuss how the items were made.

Marketing

- Exhibit samples of jewelry in a case to help draw attention to this program.

- Make a book display with suggested steampunk titles for adults or teens. The following websites have lists of titles:
    - *The Best Sci-Fi Books:* 23 Best Steampunk Books (http://best-sci-fi-books.com/23-best-steampunk-books).
    - *The New York Public Library, Steampunk:* An Introduction for Teens (https://www.nypl.org/blog/2013/05/16/steampunk-introduction -teens).

Variations by Age Groups

- *Millennials and older adults:* Use makerspaces and unique library tools for the steampunk jewelry classes. You might include a simple introduction to soldering. Gears can be soldered together and attached to chains for the necklaces. Machines to cut metal or wood can be used to stamp out gear shapes.

- *Tweens:* Offer the simple necklace making as the only activity for those who may be new to crafting and steampunk.

- *All ages:* Set up a simple walk-in craft event for making necklaces from thin velvet ribbon or cord threaded with a few charms.

SUPERHERO AND MOVIE TIE-INS

THE MARVEL AND DC COMICS machines keep interest in heroes alive through movies, TV, and Netflix. Capitalize on those interests with a night exploring the differences between Avengers and X-Men. All ages may be interested in a "Batman Day." Or take patrons through "Superhero School."

⊙ AVENGERS VERSUS X-MEN

The Avengers and the X-Men have done battle in the pages of comic books, and a lighthearted fandom program that celebrates them both while giving patrons a chance to learn more about their favorite characters is a great one-off as well as a great addition to a library comic con.

PREP TIME	LENGTH OF PROGRAM	NUMBER OF PATRONS	SUGGESTED AGE RANGE
1–2 hours	2+ hours	25	All ages

Supplies/Shopping

- Sticky notes
- Markers

Activities

- *Movie Time:* Gather any or all of the Avengers and X-Men movies for which your library has the viewing rights (or as many as you'd like) and set up a voting station so that as patrons enter your program, they can vote for which film they'd like to watch. It's always an option to have the movie playing in the background throughout the program, but if you want to make the film a focal point of the program, you can do that, too!

- *Superhero Debate:* Depending on how enthusiastic your participants are, you can hold an Avengers versus X-Men debate, but remember to keep it civil. (Honestly, it's likely that a debate will break out regardless of whether you have one planned, so be prepared to do some moderating and guide the conversation in a positive and civilized manner.)

Crafts

- *Flash Fiction!:* Have participants write a story in five hundred words or fewer that crosses over the X-Men with the Avengers. (Reading aloud is optional.)

Costumes

- Encourage participants to dress up as their favorite member of the X-Men or Avenger! (Costume contest is optional.)

Trivia and Other Free Games

- There are many options for trivia questions involving Avengers and X-Men, including rounds of "Avengers *or* X-Men?" in which participants have to determine to which group certain superheroes have pledged their allegiance, straightforward trivia questions about the comics, or questions about the movies versus the comics.

- A fun and easy game option is to provide sticky notes with names of heroes that participants stick to their foreheads and then they go around the group asking questions to determine the identity they have assumed.

Marketing

- Create a display of Avengers and X-Men comics, graphic novels, and movies, and include information about the program on the display.

◉ BATMAN DAY

Batman Day has become an annual event thanks to the folks at DC Comics, and they even provide great activity kits for libraries to use in their celebration. This program is practically planned for you!

PREP TIME	LENGTH OF PROGRAM	NUMBER OF PATRONS	SUGGESTED AGE RANGE
5 hours	Typically an all-day or half-day event with smaller programs	Unlimited, depending on space	All ages

Supplies/Shopping

- Card stock and computer paper in assorted colors
- Markers, colored pencils, crayons
- Stickers, glitter pens (optional)
- Elastic bands (for masks)
- Scissors
- Button maker and basic button-making supplies
- Batman coloring sheets (many options available for free on Pinterest)
- Batman and Batgirl mask templates (available for free on Pinterest)

Activities

- Download the activity kit from DC Comics (www.dccomics.com/blog/2016/09/01/celebrate-batman-day-on-september-17th), and make sure you are on DC's mailing list to keep updated on the next Batman Day. The kit has activities and giveaways geared mainly toward younger patrons. Don't let that deter you, though; Batman Day is for everyone!

- *Holy Movie Marathon, Batman!:* An obvious route to take is a Batman movie marathon, and due to the multiple times the Caped Crusader has graced the big screen, there is no shortage of options for viewing. See the "Variations by Age Groups" section for detailed suggestions.

- *Batman Discussion Group:* Hold a discussion of the comics and graphic novels featuring Batman, either by advertising in advance the specific run that will be discussed so participants can prepare and read the items beforehand or by having someone give a general talk about Batman's long comic history.

Crafts

- *Mask Decorating:* Set up a station where participants can color their own Batman or Batgirl mask! Using templates from online, you can precut the masks and add the elastic band ahead of time so that patrons only need to personalize their masks.

- *Button Making:* Patrons can create their own Batman buttons! As with mask decorating, it will be best to precut the pieces of paper to the correct size for your button maker so that patrons can get right to decorating. Consider providing Batman and comics stickers to be used in the buttons.

- *Batman Coloring Pages:* This is a great passive option to have available at your celebration. Simply set out the coloring pages with some markers, crayons, and colored pencils and let your patrons take it from there!

Costumes

- Hold a Batman costume contest! In the interest of fairness, you can have a contest for each age group from babies to adults.

Trivia and Other Free Games

- Trivia is a great way to engage your patrons of all ages in testing their Batman knowledge. Younger patrons can pair with their parents or try it out on their own—just make sure to have questions of varying difficulty levels.

- *Gaming:* There's no shortage of Batman-themed board and video games, whether it's Batman Sorry! or LEGO Batman on PlayStation 4.

Marketing

- Create a display of Batman graphic novels and movies, and include information on the display about Batman Day events. Depending on your library's setup, make sure you're advertising in all departments and for all ages.

- Reach out to local comic book and collectibles shops and invite them to participate in the day at the library, thereby also giving shop owners an opportunity to promote their business. Also ask if the proprietors will advertise the library's events for Batman Day in their shops and on their social media.

Variations by Age Groups

- *All ages:* Show episodes of the original TV series, which is a great intergenerational option, or episodes of the animated series, which will appeal to millennials and, of course, younger children.

- *All ages:* Have a marathon of the Tim Burton Batman movies or the Christopher Nolan trilogy, or even show Zack Snyder's *Batman v Superman*.

⚙ SUPERHERO SCHOOL

Inspire confidence in your tweens through superheroes. Connect with your young patrons on a superhero level and encourage them to take a stance against evil in your "Superhero School." Superhero School can empower tweens to be confident in themselves and their abilities. They can learn about public speaking and gain new social and life skills. Superhero School can also provide a timely opportunity for discussions about sensitive topics and charity work. This program can be a great way to connect with shy or quiet students in your community.

PREP TIME	LENGTH OF PROGRAM	NUMBER OF PATRONS	SUGGESTED AGE RANGE
2 hours	1½ hours	25	Tweens

Supplies/Shopping

- Pencils, colored pencils, crayons
- Paper
- Fashion pads
- Superhero Fruit Snacks!
- Plates
- Napkins

Activities

- *Superhero Superpowers:* Hire a professional public speaker or partner with a school counselor or speech teacher to help participants discover what makes a superhero super. Body posture, eye contact, voice volume, and more contribute to making a superhero.

- *Superhero Me!:* Have attendees make lists of answers to the following questions: What makes you a superhero? What do you like about yourself? There are no wrong answers! Participants don't have to share the answers out loud, but you can encourage them to. Another great question to include is this: What's a personal villain in your life? (Responses might include "quiet," "not good at math," etc.) Again, these answers don't have to be shared out loud and can be collected anonymously.

Crafts

- *Superhero Costume Design:* Provide fashion pads or premade dress forms for tweens to create their designs. If you have a good partnership with a local college or art school, randomly draw one of the designs and ask students to turn it into a real-life superhero costume.

- *Create a Mini Comic!:* Attendees can write themselves into a comic—defeating their shyness villain, saving the planet from pollution, or whatever they'd like.

Marketing

- Send fliers to local organizations that have students who may need a confidence boost: the YMCA and YWCA, Boys and Girls Clubs, and school counselors.

Variations by Age Groups

- This program presents a good opportunity to partner with other organizations in your community who serve special needs groups. Examples are organizations that work with adults and young adults who are facing social challenges or who fall on the autism spectrum. Read more about programming for adults facing social challenges in *A Year of Programs for Millennials and More* (ALA Editions, 2015).

AMAZINGLY VINTAGE SCI-FI

THE AMOUNT OF MATERIAL RELATING to Doctor Who, Star Trek, and Star Wars is mind-boggling. From crafts to costumes and more, these three programs will help you make these enormous fandoms into satisfied patrons.

▶ DOCTOR WHO

Time Lords, Daleks, and sonic screwdrivers . . . oh my! Doctor Who is one of the longest-running science fiction shows in history, airing since 1963 (with some breaks between seasons). Fans of all ages gravitate toward the regenerating Doctor, and the show has found itself moving from cult status to mainstream pop culture appeal since the revival of the show in 2005. Doctor Who draws in sci-fi fans young and old as he saves the day with his companions by traveling throughout time and space.

PREP TIME	LENGTH OF PROGRAM	NUMBER OF PATRONS	SUGGESTED AGE RANGE
2 hours	1 hour	20	Teens

Supplies/Shopping

- Hostess cupcakes
- Fudge marshmallow cookies
- Chocolate frosting
- Oreos
- Icing (various colors)
- Mini pretzel rods
- Mini M&Ms
- Plastic knives
- Paper plates
- Toaster oven
- Polymer clay
- Toothpicks
- Marbles
- Pens
- Keychains
- Sticky notes

Activities

- *Exterminate Daleks:* Daleks aren't so scary when they're made out of chocolate! Turn a Hostess cupcake upside down and add frosting, Oreos, and fudge marshmallow cookies for the body. Decorate with mini M&Ms, mini pretzel rods, or icing to make unique Daleks. (For instructions, see www .instructables.com/id/Mommys-mini-CHOCOLATE-DALEKS/?ALLSTEPS.)

Crafts

- *Keychains and Charms:* Use polymer clay to make charms with iconic Doctor Who references, such as the TARDIS, sonic screwdrivers, bow ties, Daleks, and the like. Heat the clay charms in the toaster oven or let them air dry. Attach to keychains.

- *Sonic Screwdriver:* Create a sonic screwdriver by decorating a simple pen with polymer clay and placing a marble at the top of one end. Take this craft a step farther by taking apart a book light and inserting the battery and light mechanism into a wide highlighter (after removing the contents of the highlighter). Use washi tape or clay to decorate.

Costumes

- Encourage attendees to dress in their best bow ties and long scarves for the occasion. Whovians are some of the most passionate fans and will come decked out in their best cosplay wear if given the opportunity.

Trivia and Other Free Games

- Doctor Who trivia can be about everything and anything in the Whovian universe, from tech toys to time and space travel to saving the world. Library staff can also separate trivia rounds by the Doctors because many attendees may be relatively new fans to the series.

- Play a Doctor Who version of "Heroes vs. Villains." Write character names on sticky notes, separated by seasons and Doctors, and have teens place the notes on their foreheads. They must ask yes or no questions to determine who their character is. It may be best to separate the seasons and Doctors because some fans will only be familiar with later seasons.

Marketing

- The TARDIS is such an iconic piece of the Doctor Who fandom that it is instantly recognizable by fans and pop culture fanatics. Make a TARDIS out of a refrigerator box, or build one if possible. This is a great way to get other departments such as maintenance or marketing engaged in library programming. Place the TARDIS in a central area of your library for maximum impact. Post a sign advertising your program and explaining what a TARDIS is for the non-Whovians. Use the TARDIS to promote your library's comic con as well!

- Promote your Doctor Who comic books in a display and insert information about the program as well.

Variations by Age Groups

- *Millennials:* Have a viewing party with themed mixed drinks for attendees who are 21 and older. Create a Sonic Screwdriver drink for millennials. Other possibilities are a TARDIS Tequila Sunrise and Cybermen Cocktails. Have attendees vote among selected fan favorite episodes on social media or your library's website. Ask patrons to bring in black T-shirts and create bleach pen fandom graphic tees. Designs can be done freehand, but it will be helpful to have templates and cutouts.

- *Older adults:* Although some older episodes may have been lost forever, some popular episodes are still available. Have a night of screenings from earlier Doctors and enjoy some crafts and snacks.

⬢ STAR TREK NIGHT

Though it's unlikely that its popularity would have waned, a cinematic reboot has ensured that Star Trek continues to be present in pop culture and that its fandom continues to grow.

PREP TIME	LENGTH OF PROGRAM	NUMBER OF PATRONS	SUGGESTED AGE RANGE
4 hours	2 hours	Unlimited, depending on space	All ages

Supplies/Shopping

- Star Trek coloring sheets
- Crayons, colored pencils

Activities

- *Golden Oldies Night:* If possible, show some episodes of the original Star Trek series, or perhaps one of the original movies as well as one of the new ones.

- *Meet a Superfan:* Contact a local Star Trek superfan and ask the person to lead a discussion or give a talk about a particular aspect of the series. For leads, contact your local comics shop or gaming store.

- *Star Trek Science:* Invite a local astronomy or science professor to talk science fact.

Crafts

- *Coloring Pages:* Provide Star Trek coloring sheets so that even the youngest Trekkies can participate.

Costumes

- Costumes should absolutely be encouraged!

Trivia and Other Free Games

- Consider holding a trivia tournament, though be sure to clarify to which specific series the questions will refer.

Marketing

- Create a display of Star Trek DVDs as well as fiction and nonfiction books, and include information about the program.

Variations by Age Groups

- None necessary

⭐ STAR WARS: MAY THE FOURTH BE WITH YOU AND FREE COMIC BOOK DAY

Free Comic Book Day occurs yearly on the first Saturday of May. This event occasionally coincides with Star Wars Day, which is, of course, May the Fourth. When both observances occur on the same date, it presents an especially great opportunity to hold a joint celebration. Even when these two events don't fall on the same day, they still present a wealth of programming opportunities.

PREP TIME	LENGTH OF PROGRAM	NUMBER OF PATRONS	SUGGESTED AGE RANGE
5+ hours (depending on how involved your program is)	3 hours	Unlimited, depending on space	All ages

Supplies/Shopping

- Coloring pages from Star Wars or comic books
- Markers, crayons, colored pencils
- Star Wars video games
- Superhero and Star Wars picture books

Activities

- *Drawing Demo:* Invite a local artist, especially one who has done comic book work or is familiar with character drawing, to do a drawing demonstration or workshop.
- *Video Gaming:* Set up video gaming stations at which attendees can play various Star Wars video games, such as LEGO Star Wars.
- *Superhero and Star Wars Storytime:* There is a wealth of superhero and Star Wars picture books, so invite one of your children's librarians to hold a special storytime.

Crafts

- *Coloring Time:* Provide Star Wars and comic book coloring pages so even the youngest fans can show their fandom!

Costumes

- Costumes should absolutely be encouraged!

Trivia and Other Free Games

- Consider having all-ages Star Wars trivia—though you'll want to specify which parts of the Star Wars universe you'll be covering (the original trilogy, all of the movies, the expanded universe books, etc.).

Marketing

- Talk to your local comic shop operators about their plans for Free Comic Book Day. Often, they will be willing to help acquire comic books from publishers that you can give away at your library. They might also be interested in setting up a table at your Free Comic Book Day celebration (providing library administration is okay with this). Your local shops will, of course, also be holding their own celebrations, so the key here is not to split the audience but, rather, to celebrate comic books across your community. Make sure to give your local shops a shout-out at your Free Comic Book Day celebration.

- Create a display of Star Wars books, graphic novels, movies, and games, and include information about the program on the display. Be sure to visit the Free Comic Book Day site to download the logo for your Free Comic Book Day promotion as well. If your local comic shops will be participating on-site, be sure to include them in your promotions!

Variations by Age Groups

Because this program is intended for all ages, variations are not necessary, but it is worth noting that some libraries choose to hold their library comic con on Free Comic Book Day or on May the Fourth. If your library would like to hold its first comic con but is unsure about the date or how large the program should be, consider pairing your library comic con with a celebration like this. Be advised, though, that because of other events on the same day, potential local partners and artists might not be available to participate in your comic con if you hold it on Free Comic Book Day.

COMIC CON

COMIC CONS ARE AMONG THE most popular library fandom events, with many systems offering entire days of activities or a month containing themed events. Although the "Cape and Mask Design" and "Costume Contests" programs listed in this section may be simple and familiar, the other programs are more elaborate. "Action Figures Assemble" provides ideas for recycling toy action figures or using them with technology in the library. The "Art and Collector Fest" will inspire creativity and attract fans, while "Fandom Frenzy" offers several energetic, comics-themed ideas to build on.

⊙ ACTION FIGURES ASSEMBLE

This series of activities will show participants how to repurpose action figures. These activities are meant to take place over a series of days or with different age groups. Asking for donations of old action figures in the weeks before the program will ensure that there is a plentiful supply. Well-loved plastic heroes with missing parts can also be included.

PREP TIME	LENGTH OF PROGRAM	NUMBER OF PATRONS	SUGGESTED AGE RANGE
2 hours for several activities	1 hour for most activities	15–25 for craft activities	Millennials

Supplies/Shopping

STOP-MOTION ANIMATION STATION

- iPad (loaded with a stop-motion app)
- Tripod (optional)

JEWELRY AND KEYCHAINS

- Eye screws
- Lighter
- Jump rings
- Ball chains or thin leather cord necklaces
- Long- and short-nose pliers

TERRARIUMS

- Small glass or plastic containers
- Stones (varying sizes)
- Moss
- Silk leaves and twigs

ACTION FIGURE LAMPS

- Inexpensive lamps (purchase at a thrift or discount store)
- Metallic spray acrylic paint
- Super Glue

Activities

- *Collecting Action Figures:* Invite an expert on collecting toys to talk about value and ways to sell collections. Hold a collectors' fair and invite people with collections to set up tables at which attendees can buy items or bring some to sell. This activity also crosses over with the My Little Pony, Star Wars, Star Trek, and Doctor Who events in this book.

- *Stop-Motion Animation Station:* Set up a scene in a makerspace or a place where attendees can try some stop-motion animation. This activity will require an iPad loaded with an app for stop-motion animation and likely a tripod. The following resources offer suggestions along with tips on how to keep the station useful and low maintenance:
    - ‣ Teen Librarian Toolbox, Take 5: Stop Motion Animation Hacks for a MakerSpace (www.teenlibrariantoolbox.com/2015/12take-5-stop-motion-animation-hacks-for-a-makerspace).
    - ‣ Library as Makerspace, DIY Club: Stop Motion Month (http://librarymakerspace.blogspot.com/2014/10/diy-club-stop-motion-month.html).

Crafts

- *Terrariums:* Provide a variety of small glass or plastic containers, stones of different sizes, moss, silk leaves, and twigs so participants can set up scenes with action figures in their fake terrarium. This craft also can be done with real plants, soil, and natural elements, but the containers must allow for watering.

- *Keychains or Jewelry:* Many tiny action figures can be attached to leather cords or ball chains with jump rings. Larger figures can be attached with eye screws and a lighter. Using the lighter, heat the eye screw until it can be inserted into the rubber action figure before attaching jump rings and cords. These figures can also be attached to keychain hardware.

- *Action Figure Lamps:* This craft requires ventilation. Using Super Glue, attach action figures around a lamp base in a layered, dimensional sculpture. Coat the base well with metallic spray paint.

Costumes

- *Wonder Twins:* Patrons who send or bring in photos (either present or past) of themselves dressed like their action figure will win a prize. This activity will also help advertise the program.

Trivia and Other Free Games

- *Hot Collectibles:* In a case, display collectible action figures with cards revealing how much the figures sell for on eBay. Ask questions about collectible or unusual figures on a trivia sheet that people can turn in or answer online to enter a drawing for a prize. This is a crossover event with the My Little Pony, Star Wars, Star Trek, or Doctor Who events.

Marketing

- Place action figures holding signs about the program by a display of graphic novels or on a smaller scale at each lane at the circulation desk.

- *Not Elf on a Shelf:* Advertise that an action figure will be hiding in a particular collection once a day or periodically throughout the month during which comics or action figure programs will be held. The winner can receive candy. This is a good way to send patrons to little-known areas of the library. Be sure not to hide the figures too well or patrons may mess up the collection trying to find them.

Variations by Age Groups

- *All ages—Story Contest:* Set up a scene with action figures and take a photo. Enlarge the photo (or make the scene visible but sealed off behind glass) and let patrons fill out a sticky note or a paper slip explaining what is happening in the scene. Stipulations about G-rated content make this an event for all ages.

- *All ages—Photo Contest in the Library:* Another G-rated event with published rules, this photo contest for patrons to do in the library can be a fun way to use the donated old figures. Invite everyone to pose with an action figure or show one using the library.

- *Older adults:* The "Collecting Action Figures" activity is also suitable for this age group.

ART AND COLLECTOR FEST

One of the best parts of any comic con is getting to visit the Artists' Alley and meet comic book writers and artists. Depending on your location and access to local talent, you can incorporate an Artists' Alley (henceforth referred to as an Art and Collector Fest) at your library mini con. You can also reach out to local collectors (comic book or otherwise) and give them an opportunity to show off their collections. Your mini con attendees will be awed and inspired—and perhaps even surprised—after taking a stroll through your Art and Collector Fest.

Prep Time

Begin preparations several months in advance of your event in order to find creators who are available.

LENGTH OF PROGRAM	NUMBER OF PATRONS	SUGGESTED AGE RANGE
Generally 2–3 hours, but can be longer!	Unlimited, depending on space	All ages

Supplies/Shopping

- No shopping is required for this program, but make sure you have tables, chairs, and adequate space for your Fest!

Activities

- *Panel Discussion:* In addition to having artists and collectors set up at tables to display their work, ask whether any are interested in participating in a panel discussion about their experiences, influences, methods, and so on. Depending on how many artists and collectors are participating in the con, you can form smaller groups of panelists and hold separate theme-related discussions.

- *Drawing Workshop:* Because they'll be at the con anyway, ask whether any of the artists are interested in leading a drawing workshop. This activity applies to writers as well, and if any collectors present have a particular niche collection (say, Star Wars toys or Wonder Woman comic books), see if they would be interested in holding a more in-depth informational or question-and-answer session about their collection.

PRO TIP

Find out whether your artists and collectors have their own signage (if they regularly set up at cons, chances are they will). If they don't, make sure to provide signage indicating the artist's or collector's name and specialty.

Crafts

- *Comic and Zine Creation Station:* Set up an area in which participants can make their own comics and zines (see the "Zine Workshop" description for details).

Marketing

- Reach out to local comic book and collectibles shops for leads on artists and collectors in the area, and ask about hanging fliers or posting information in the shops. An Art and Collector Fest isn't the same thing as a vendor fair, but perhaps you can also ask local shop proprietors if they would like to set up and sell (pending approval from your library, of course; every library has different rules about selling merchandise on library property).

Variations by Age Groups

Variations aren't necessary for this program, but a good rule of thumb is to make sure you have family-friendly content represented in your Fest. This isn't to say that all your artists and collectors must appeal strictly to children but, rather, that the art and collectibles represented are appropriate for a public library setting.

⚙ CAPE AND MASK DESIGN

Cape and mask design programs can be very simple and inexpensive or elaborate. The crafts involved can range from drawing with permanent markers on premade masks and capes to using glitter and feathers for the masks to sewing for the capes. This program can be run as a drop-in event as part of a bigger comics festival or as a scheduled, preregistered event.

PREP TIME	LENGTH OF PROGRAM	NUMBER OF PATRONS	SUGGESTED AGE RANGE
30 minutes	45 minutes	20	11+ (all ages)

Supplies/Shopping

- Scissors
- Fabric and craft glue
- Permanent markers
- Table coverings
- Feathers
- Stick-on gems
- Plain masks (white, black, or colors; available at dollar stores, party suppliers, etc.)
- Capes to decorate (available at dollar stores or online craft and party stores) or felt or satin to cut and make capes, adhesive Velcro dots, fusible hem tape, ¾-inch ribbon (27 inches per registered patron)
- Iron-on printer transfer paper or purchased superhero logo iron-on transfers
- Felt or lightweight fleece (to make decorative shapes and patches)
- Fabric paint (acrylic, dimensional, and traditional)

Activities

- *One month before:* Shop for supplies online or in person to be sure you will have enough on hand. Also contact staff at a local craft store to see if they would be willing to present ideas for participants.

- *1 hour before:* Set up stations for different decorating techniques. For example, cover all tables that will have markers, paints, and glue. If an ironing board is needed, set that up near an outlet. A laptop and ink-jet printer can be set up for doing iron-on transfers. If sewing will be done, designate an area for hand sewing with needles or a station with machines, thread, and scissors. Be sure to have plenty of garbage cans available in the room. Demonstrate each technique and let participants choose the way they want to work on their project.

- *Masks:* Masks can be easily made with felt, a small hole punch, and elastic cord. They can be decorated with glitter glue and markers but will not be washable.

Trivia and Other Free Games

- Begin the program by showing masked characters from past decades for examples and for fun trivia.

Marketing

- Encourage staff to wear capes as a fun way to advertise this program.
- Display capes and masks with information about the program.

Variations by Age Groups

- *Tweens, teens, and millennials:* These groups may appreciate entire costume workshops that can include fashioning boots or shoes from duct tape, making basic weapons out of cardboard, and face painting for popular cosplay characters from books. If a movie is coming out around the time of the planned program, provide online tutorials about these elements.

- *Teens and millennials:* Have attendees use dimensional fabric paint or hot glue to outline a mask pattern drawn in pencil on tracing paper. When dry, the paint or glue outline will peel off to form a three-dimensional, cob-web-like mask. For wearing, attach ribbons to avoid stretching the fragile mask.

- *Millennials—Masquerade Masks:* Set up a mask-making makerspace for Mardi Gras. This activity can also work for the "Time Travel" program.

- *Older adults:* An introductory costume-making course that involves basic hand or machine sewing on simple seams will appeal to this group. Adults who want to make costumes for children can learn how to copy popular costumes simply. Invite employees from area thrift stores and craft or fabric shops to lead these workshops on inexpensive, easy costuming.

✪ COSTUME CONTESTS

As mentioned in the "Tips and Tricks for Fandom Events" section of this book, cosplay and costumes are no longer popular just with young children. Patterns are available to make easy costumes for many popular characters or types or periods. The library can offer classes in simple robe making for a Harry Potter program or accessory design for a steampunk or superhero event, but having costume contests is a way to include adults who purchase their costumes. Prizes need not be expensive, and patrons throughout the library may enjoy seeing the costumes on parade.

PREP TIME	LENGTH OF PROGRAM	NUMBER OF PATRONS	SUGGESTED AGE RANGE
1 hour	30–45 minutes	Unlimited	Teens and millennials

Supplies/Shopping

- Prizes (optional)

Activities

- *Parade:* Although a parade of costumed participants in the library is fun, consider partnering with another community agency to host a larger event. If weather is a concern, perhaps a large mall or a park district facility may work. Offer prizes by ages and include a number of ways to win—for example, best character from a book, best action hero, best costume by age group, and most creative.

- *Costume Party:* A library costume event to end a comic festival would be fun. Separate age groups into different rooms or stagger attendance times, and provide light refreshments, photos, photo booths, coloring sheets, and movies before awards are given. Invite participants to discuss their costumes, highlighting how the costumes were made, if applicable. Feature winning costumes in a poster advertising the library.

- *Online:* In the weeks before the event, invite participants to send in costume photos by age and theme with an explanation of how the costumes were made.

- *Pet Costumes:* Hold a small pet parade in the library. Require prior registration, and establish rules to keep the event controlled. Patrons can also send in photos for an online pet costume contest, with categories that include pet owners.

Crafts

- *Costume Elements:* Ask contest winners to host another program detailing how they designed some of the elements of their costumes.

- *Makeup:* Have a costume makeup expert give tips or set up a station for patrons who attend but may want help with a costume.

Trivia and Other Free Games

- *Character Costume ID:* While people are arriving for the parade or the party, show photos of parts of costumes worn by famous characters and ask audience members to identify the characters.

Marketing

- Post pictures of costumes from past events or from current ones if patrons send in their pictures ahead of time.

- Dress a puppet or stuffed animal in a simple costume and use photos of the critter on publicity materials.

FANDOM FRENZY

Bringing together fans who span generations, species, and sometimes the space-time continuum is part of what makes a comic con unique. Part of the joy of a comic con is owning and sharing your nerdom with like-minded friends and potentially finding new ones. Hanging out and geeking out among peers allows one to express one's inner fangirl or fanboy, debate passionately, and learn about new, exciting fandoms.

A "Fandom Frenzy" is an open forum that allows people to gather and let their nerd flag fly! Have icebreakers and activities ready to get people chatting about their fandom. At the end of the program, it is hoped, patrons will have discovered new friends and fandoms to explore.

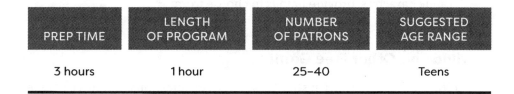

PREP TIME	LENGTH OF PROGRAM	NUMBER OF PATRONS	SUGGESTED AGE RANGE
3 hours	1 hour	25–40	Teens

Supplies/Shopping

- Clear plastic cups
- Paper table coverings
- Sharpies (assorted colors)
- Laptop
- Projector
- Microphone
- Fandom snack or drink ingredients
- Costumes

Activities

- *DIY Movieoke:* Find fan favorites of heartbreaking and hilarious scenes and give teens a microphone to act them out. Add closed captions, mute the voices, and challenge teens to reenact the scenes. If some attendees aren't fans, pair a fan with a non-fan and let the hilarity roll!

- *Speed Fandoming:* Have teens explain their fandom in ninety seconds or less. This activity can be done in pairs or in groups. Mash up characters from different fandoms and put them into random scenarios.

- *Fan Fare:* Have the group make a fandom-themed beverage or snack, and tie it into a recent media release (for example, Ecto Coolers from *Ghostbusters*, butterbeer from Harry Potter, and snow cones from *Frozen*).

Crafts

- *Fan Art*: Many people use art as a way to express themselves and show their allegiance to particular fandoms. Set out colored Sharpies for teens to decorate paper-covered tables and plastic cups with favorite characters, symbols, and signs.

Costumes

- *Costume Grab Bag*: Raid your costume closet from past programs and storytelling events. Write fandoms and character names on pieces of paper. Form teams and have each team choose one piece of paper. Teams will then attempt to emulate the fandom or character by putting together costumes from the leftover scraps. Have all the teams guess what character or fandom each costume represents. If teens have trouble guessing fandoms and characters, provide names to choose from.

Trivia and Other Free Games

- *Decisions Icebreaker*: On slips of paper, write questions that force people to choose between two actions or characters—for example, "Would you rather have to always wear an invisibility cloak or be permanently transfigured into a shark's head?" or "Would you rather turn into a raging Hulk every time you get angry or be permanently blue?" Have each teen draw one question and then read the question and give the answer out loud either in small groups or for the whole group.

- *Trivia PowerPoint*: Create a trivia PowerPoint that has rounds from various fandoms and that will reach a wide audience. Include questions about fandom lifestyles that are generic and apply to all fandoms, such as, "What does OTP stand for?" or "What are two websites on which you can share fan art?" (Answers: OTP = One True Pair; Deviant Art and Tumblr, among many).

Marketing

- Include "Fandom Frenzy" as one part of the comic con day. Emphasize opportunities to hang out and meet up with fellow fans and nerds.

- Promote "Fandom Frenzy" in already popular fandom books at the library.

- Use memes and fandom characters on posters to promote the event, if copyright allows.

- Many fans live their fandom life in online communities and through social media. Reach out to them where they already are and advertise on social media, book blogs, fan art sites, and Tumblr.

Variations by Age Groups

- *Tweens:* Many tweens will enjoy these activities as well but may want the activities to be more focused on specific fandoms, such as superheroes.

- *Millennials:* Focus on fandoms that have particular meaning and appeal for the millennial generation or that are going through a pop culture revival near the time of your program. If your library allows alcohol to be served and consumed on-site, consider creating a Random Fandom Beverage inspired by your favorite fandom, such as a "Jar-Jar I Don't Think So" drink from the Cantina of the Star Wars universe.

- *Millennials:* Re-create an iconic location from a favorite 1990s TV show or movie for photo opportunities.

- *Millennials:* Theme your trivia to include popular 1980s and '90s highlights. Include music, movies, fashion, and news rounds from the 1980s and '90s that will tug on millennials' nostalgic memories.

ABOUT THE AUTHORS

AMY J. ALESSIO is an award-winning librarian with a black belt in karate. She is the coauthor of *A Year of Programs for Millennials and More* (ALA Editions, 2015) and *Club Programs for Teens* (ALA Editions, 2015). She teaches graduate-level young adult literature and conducts dozens of webinars every year, including ones on the topic of social media for book lovers. Amy enjoys sharing her passion for Jell-O and kolackies with thirty local and national audiences a year during interactive presentations on vintage cookbooks and crafts. She reviews romance titles for *Booklist* and has written and edited several works of fiction and nonfiction. She is a former board member for the Young Adult Library Services Association. Learn more at www.amyalessio.com.

KATIE LaMANTIA is a teen librarian at the Schaumburg Township District Library in Schaumburg, Illinois. She is a former Teen Advisory Board member turned teen librarian and is the coauthor of *A Year of Programs for Millennials and More* (ALA Editions, 2015). She has a personal and professional appreciation for and interest in pop culture and has presented at multiple state and national library conferences about libraries, teens, and programming for adults in their 20s and 30s. When not running teen programs, tinkering with technology, and finding books for young adults, she enjoys traveling, reading, writing, and extreme adventure activities.

EMILY VINCI is an adult fiction librarian at the Schaumburg Township District Library in Schaumburg, Illinois, where she cofounded NextGen, a social group for people in their 20s and 30s. She has presented many times about building great programs for patrons in their 20s and 30s and coauthored *A Year of Programs for Millennials and More* (ALA Editions, 2015). She is passionate about expanding librarian and patron appreciation for and knowledge of comics and graphic novels. A pop culture fanatic, she is always looking for new ways to incorporate popular culture into the public library. When she isn't working, she can usually be found reading comic books, watching movies, or curating her many collections—especially those of *Jaws* and *Jurassic Park* memorabilia.

INDEX